SELECTED POEMS

of

Edwin Arlington Robinson

SELECTED POEMS

of

Edwin Arlington Robinson

EDITED BY

MORTON DAUWEN ZABEL

With an introduction by James Dickey

MACMILLAN PUBLISHING COMPANY
NEW YORK

COLLIER MACMILLAN PUBLISHERS
LONDON

Macmillan Publishing Company
866 Third Avenue, New York, NY 10022
Collier Macmillan Canada, Inc.

Library of Congress Cataloging-in-Publication Data
Robinson, Edwin Arlington, 1869–1935.
    [Poems. Selections]
    Selected poems of Edwin Arlington Robinson / edited by Morton
Dauwen Zabel ; with an introduction by James Dickey.—
1st Hudson River ed.
      p. cm.
    Includes bibliographical references.
    ISBN 0-02-604081-6
    I. Zabel, Morton Dauwen, 1901–1964. II. Title.
PS3535.025A17   1989
811'.52—dc20   89-12722   CIP

Macmillan books are available at special discounts for bulk purchases
for sales promotions, premiums, fund-raising, or educational use.
For details, contact:

> Special Sales Director
> Macmillan Publishing Company
> 866 Third Avenue
> New York, NY 10022

FIRST HUDSON RIVER EDITION 1989

10 9 8 7 6 5 4 3 2 1

PRINTED IN THE UNITED STATES OF AMERICA

Contents

From THE MAN AGAINST THE SKY (1916)   99

Introduction

EDWIN ARLINGTON ROBINSON: THE MANY TRUTHS

A reevaluation of the work of a poet as established as Edwin Arlington Robinson should involve us in some of the fundamentals we tend to forget when we read any poetry that happens to come to hand—the poetry that is thrust upon us by critics and in courses in literature as well as the poetry that we seek out or return to. As should be true of our encounter with any poetry, reevaluation requires that we rid ourselves of preconceptions and achieve, if we can, a way of reading an established poet as though we had never heard of him and were opening his book for the first time. It requires that we approach him with all our senses open, our intelligence in acute readiness, our critical sense in check but alert for the slightest nuance of falsity, our truth-sensitive needle—the device that measures what the poet says against what we know from having lived it—at its most delicate, and our sense of the poet's "place," as determined by commentary, textbook, and literary fashion, drugged, asleep, or temporarily dead.

Like most ideal conditions, this one cannot be fully attained. But it is certainly true that an approximation of such a state is both an advantage and a condition productive of unsuspected discoveries in reading poets we thought we knew, particularly poets whom we thought we knew as well as Robinson. In Robinson's special case it is even more difficult than usual, for the course of poetry has to a certain extent turned away from him, making his greatest virtues appear mediocre ones and directing public scrutiny from his introspective, intellectual, and ironic toward poetry in which more things seem to be taking place in a smaller area—poetry in which the poetic line is compressed and packed to the point of explosion and the bedazzlement of the reader is considered synonymous with his reward.

Robinson achieved unusual popularity in his lifetime. When he died in 1935, at the age of sixty-five, he had won the Pulitzer Prize three times and had gained a distinction rare for a poet—his book-length poem *Tristram* had become a best seller. But in the public mind, Robinson has during recent years been regarded as only his vices of prolixity, irresolution, and occasional dullness would have him. Yet if we could manage to read Robinson as if we did not know him—or at least as if we did not know him quite so well as we had believed—or if we could come to him as if he were worth rereading, not out of duty and obedience to literary history but as a possible experience, we would certainly gain a good deal more than we would lose.

I

Suppose, eager only for the experience of poems, we were to look through this book before reading it, noting only the shapes of the poems on the page. We would see a good many short, tight-looking poems in different structural forms, all of them severely symmetrical, and page after page containing long vertical rectangles of blank verse. Though this selection leaves out the Arthurian poems on which Robinson's popular reputation was made as well as the other later narratives of his declining years, there are still a number of middling-long poems that no editor interested in Robinson's best work could possibly eliminate. The chances are that we would be inclined to skip these and first read one of the shorter ones. What would we find if it were this one?

> We go no more to Calverly's,
> For there the lights are few and low;
> And who are there to see by them,
> Or what they see, we do not know.
> Poor strangers of another tongue
> May now creep in from anywhere,
> And we, forgotten, be no more
> Than twilight on a ruin there.
>
> We two, the remnant. All the rest
> Are cold and quiet. You nor I,
> Nor fiddle now, nor flagon-lid,
> May ring them back from where they lie.
> No fame delays oblivion
> For them, but something yet survives:
> A record written fair, could we
> But read the book of scattered lives.
>
> There'll be a page for Leffingwell,
> And one for Lingard, the Moon-calf;

And who knows what for Clavering,
Who died because he couldn't laugh?
Who knows or cares? No sign is here,
No face, no voice, no memory;
No Lingard with his eerie joy,
No Clavering, no Calverly.

We cannot have them here with us
To say where their light lives are gone,
Or if they be of other stuff
Than are the moons of Ilion.
So, be their place of one estate
With ashes, echoes, and old wars—
Or ever we be of the night,
Or we be lost among the stars.

It is a poem that opens, conventionally enough, with a reference to a place—one suspects from the beginning that it is one of those drinking places where men gather against the dark and call it fellowship—where there were once parties or at least conviviality of some sort; of that company, only two are left, and one of these is speaking. We feel the conventionality of the theme because we are aware that the contrast between places formerly full of animation and merriment with the same places *now* is one of the most haggard of romantic clichés and the subject of innumerable mediocre verses (though infrequently, as in some of Hardy, it can be memorable and can serve to remind us that such contrasts, such places, do in fact exist and *are* melancholy and cautionary). Yet there is a difference, a departure, slight but definitive, from the conventional. This difference begins to become apparent as we read the last two stanzas, which are mainly a roll call of the missing. The Robinsonian departure is in the way in which these dead are characterized. What, for example, are we to make of the reference to "Clavering/Who died because he couldn't laugh?" Or of "Lingard with his eerie joy"? What of these people, here barely mentioned, but mentioned in connection with tantalizing qualities that are hard to forget, that have in them some of the inexplicably sad individuality that might be—that might as well be—fate? I suspect that one who began as even the most casual reader might wish to know more of these people, and he might then realize that in Robinson's other poems, and only there, he would have a chance of doing so.

A first perusal of "Calverly's" might also lead the perceptive reader to suspect that the poet is more interested in the human personality than he is in, say, nature; that he is interested in people not only for their enigmatic and haunting qualities but also for their mysterious exemplification of some larger entity, some agency that, though it determines both their lives and their deaths, may or may not have any concern for them or knowledge of them. Of these men, the poet cannot say "where their light lives are gone," and because he cannot say—and because there is nothing or no way to tell him—he cannot know, either, what his own fate is, or its meaning; he can know only that he himself was once at Calverly's, that the others who were there are gone, and that he shall follow them in due time. He cannot say what this means or whether, in fact, it means anything. Though he can guess as to what it might mean, all he finally *knows* is what has happened.

This condition of mind is a constant throughout all but a very few of Robinson's poems. It links him in certain curious ways with the existentialists, but we are aware of such affinities only tangentially, for Robinson's writings, whatever else they may be, are dramas that make use of conjecture rather than overt statements of ideas held and defended. It is the fact that truth is "so strange in its nakedness" that appalled and intrigued him—the fact that it takes different forms for different people and different situations. Robinson believed in the unknowable constants that govern the human being from within; in addition, he had the sort of mind that sees history as a unity in which these human constants appear in dramatic form. This explains why he had no difficulty at all in projecting Welsh kingdoms and biblical encounters out of houses and situations he had known in New England, much as his own Shakespeare was able to fill "Ilion, Rome, or any town you like/Of olden time with timeless Englishmen."

The unity of the poet's mind is a quality that is certain to make its presence felt very early in the reader's acquaintance with Robinson. One can tell a great deal about him from the reading of a single poem. All the poems partake of a single view and a single personality, and one has no trouble in associating the poems in strict forms with the more irregular ones as the products of the same vision of existence. The sensibility evidenced by the poems is both devious and tenacious, and it lives most intensely when unresolved about questions dealing with the human personality. Robinson is perhaps the greatest master of the speculative or conjectural approach to the writing of poetry. Uncertainty was the air he breathed, and speculation was not so much a device with him—though at its best it is a surpassingly effective technique—as it was a habit of mind, an integral part of the self. As with most powerful poets, the writing proceeded from the way in which Robinson naturally thought, the way he naturally *was,* and so was inextricably rooted in his reticent, slightly morbid, profoundly contemplative, solitary, compassionate, and stoical personality and was not the product of a conscious search for a literary "way," an unusual manner of speaking which was invented or discovered and in which the will had a major part.

Robinson's tentative point of view was solidly wedded to a style that has exactly the same characteritics as his mind. It makes an artistic virtue, and often a very great one, of arriving at only provisional answers and solutions, of leaving it up to the reader's personality—also fated—to choose from among them the most likely. Thus a salient quality of Robinson's work is the extraordinary roundness and fullness he obtains from such circumlocutions of his subjects, as though he were indeed turning (in William James's phrase) "the cube of reality." One is left with the belief that in any given situation there are many truths—as many, so to speak, as there are persons involved, as there are witnesses, as there are ways of thinking about it. And encompassing all these is the shadowy probability that none of them is or can be final. What we see in Robinson's work is the unending and obsessional effort to make sense of experience when perhaps there is none to be made. The poet, the reader, all of us are members of humanity in the sense Robinson intended when he characterized the earth as "a kind of vast spiritual kindergarten where millions of people are trying to spell God with the wrong blocks."

It is through people that Robinson found the hints and gleams of the universal condition that he could not help trying to solve. Like other human beings, he was cursed with intelligence and sensibility in a universe made for material objects. "The world is a hell of a place," he once said, "but the universe is a fine thing," and again, "We die of what we eat and drink,/But more we die of what we think." Robinson has been perhaps the only American poet—certainly the only one of major status—interested *exclusively* in human beings as subject matter for poetry—in the psychological, motivational aspects of living, in the inner life as it is projected upon the outer. His work is one vast attempt to tell the stories that no man can really tell, for no man can know their real meaning, their real intention, or even whether such exists, though it persistently appears to do so. In all Robinson's people the Cosmos seems to be brooding in one way or another, so that a man and woman sitting in a garden, as in "Mortmain," are, in *what* they are, exemplars of eternal laws that we may guess at but not know. The laws are present in psychological constitutions as surely as they are in physical materials, in the orbital patterns of stars and planets and atoms, only deeper hid, more tragic and mysterious, "as there might somewhere be veiled/Eternal reasons why the tricks of time/Were played like this."

Robinson wrote an enormous amount of poetry (how one's mind quails at the sheer *weight*, the physical bulk, of his fifteen-hundred-page *Collected Poems!*), but at the center of it and all through it is the Personality, the Mind, conditioned by its accidental placement in time and space—these give the individuations that make drama possible—but also partaking of the hidden universals, the not-to-be-knowns that torment all men. In these poems "The strange and unremembered light/That is in dreams" plays over "The nameless and eternal tragedies/That render hope and hopelessness akin." Like a man speaking under torture—or self-torture—Robinson tells of these things, circling them, painfully shifting from one possible interpretation to another, and the reader circles with him, making, for want of any received, definitive opinion, hesitant, troubling, tentative judgments. The result is an unresolved view, but a view of remarkable richness and suggestibility, opening out in many directions and unsealing many avenues of possibility: a multidimensional view that the reader is left pondering as the poem has pondered, newly aware of his own enigmas, of what he and his own life—its incidents and fatalities—may mean, could mean, and thus he is likely to feel himself linked into the insoluble universal equation, in which nature itself is only a frame of mind, a projection of inwardness, tormenting irresolution, and occasional inexplicable calms.

> . . . she could look
> Right forward through the years, nor any more
> Shrink with a cringing prescience to behold
> The glitter of dead summer on the grass,
> Or the brown-glimmered crimson of still trees
> Across the intervale where flashed along,
> Black-silvered, the cold river.

II

As has been said, Robinson's method—which on some fronts has been labeled antipoetic—would not amount to as much as it does were not the modes of thought presented in such powerful and disturbing dramatic forms. For an "antipoet," Robinson was an astonishing craftsman. One has only to read a few of his better poems in the classic French repetitive forms, such as "The House on the Hill," to recognize the part that traditional verse patterns play in his work. This much is demonstrable. It is among those who believe the poetic essence to lie somewhere outside or beyond such considerations, somewhere in the image-making, visual, and visionary realm, that Robinson's position has been challenged. And it is true that his verse is oddly bare, that there are few images in it—though, of these, some are very fine indeed—and that most of it is highly cerebral and often written in a scholarly or pseudoscholarly manner that is frequently more than a little pedantic. Many of his poems contain an element of self-parody, and these carry more than their share of bad, flat, stuffy writing.

> There were slaves who dragged the shackles of a precedent unbroken,
> Demonstrating the fulfillment of unalterable schemes,
> Which had been, before the cradle, Time's inexorable tenants
> Of what were now the dusty ruins of their fathers' dreams.

Infrequently there is also a kind of belaboring-beyond-belaboring of the obvious:

> The four square somber things that you see first
> Around you are four walls that go as high
> As to the ceiling.

And now and then one comes on philosophical pronouncements of a remarkable unconvincingness, demonstrating a total failure of idiom, of art:

> Too much of that
> May lead you by and by through gloomy lanes
> To a sad wilderness, where one may grope
> Alone, and always, or until he feels
> Ferocious and invisible animals
> That wait for men and eat them in the dark.

At his worst, Robinson seems to go on writing long after whatever he has had to say about the subject has been exhausted; there is a suspicious look of automatism about his verse instrument. The reader, being made of less stern stuff, will almost always fail before Robinson's blank verse does.

Robinson certainly wrote too much. Like Wordsworth—even more than Wordsworth, if that is possible—he is in need of selective editing. In the present book, this is what the late Morton Dauwen Zabel has done, and I believe with singular success. The Robinson of this book is much more nearly the essential, the permanently valuable Robinson than the Robinson of the *Collected Poems,* though there are unavoidable exclusions—particularly of the good book-length poems, such as *Lancelot* and *Merlin*—which one might legitimately regret and to which it is hoped that the reader will eventually have recourse. Yet even in the present volume one is likely to be put off by the length of many of the pieces. Then, too, if the casual reader skims only a little of a particular poem and finds that nothing much is happening or that event, action, and resolution are taking place only in various persons' minds, he is also likely to shy away. But once *in* the poem, committed to it, with his mind winding among the alternative complexities of Robinson's characters' minds—that is, winding with Robinson's mind—the reader changes slowly, for Robinson hath his will. One is held by the curious dry magic that seems so eminently unmagical, that bears no resemblance to the elfin or purely verbal or native-woodnote magic for which English verse is justly celebrated. It is a magic for which there is very little precedent in all literature. Though external affinities may be asserted and even partially demonstrated with Praed and Browning, though there are occasional distant echoes of Wordsworth, Keats, Hardy, and Rossetti, Robinson is really like none of them in his root qualities; his spell is cast with none of the traditional paraphernalia, but largely through his own reading of character and situation and fate, his adaptation of traditional poetic devices to serve these needs—an adaptation so unexpected, so revolutionary, as to seem not so much adaptation as transformation.

Another odd thing about Robinson is that his best work and his worst are yet remarkably alike. The qualities that make the good poems good are the same qualities that make the bad poems bad; it is only a question of how Robinson's method works out in, "takes to," the situation he is depicting, and often the difference between good, bad, and mediocre is thin indeed. This difficulty is also compounded by the fact that Robinson is equally skilled as a technician in both memorable poems and trivial ones. In the less interesting poems, particularly the longer ones, Robinson's air of portentousness can be tiresome. Reading these, one is tempted to say that Robinson is the most prolific *reticent* poet in history. Though he gives the impression that he is reluctant to write down what he is writing, he often goes on and on, in a kind of intelligent mumbling, a poetical wringing of the hands, until the reader becomes restive and a little irritated. In these passages, Robinson's verse instrument has a certain kinship with the salt maker in the fairy tale, grinding away of its own accord at the bottom of the sea. Then there is the gray, austere landscape of the poems, the lack of background definition. One is accustomed to finding the characters in a poem—particularly a narrative poem—in a *place*, a location with objects and a weather of its own, a world which the reader can enter and in which he can, as it were, live with the characters. But there is very little of the environmental in Robinson's work. What few gestures and concessions he makes to the outside world are token ones; all externality is quickly devoured by the tormented introversion of his personages. In Robinson, the mind eats everything and converts it to part of a conflict with self; one could say with some justification that all Robinson's poems are about people who are unable to endure themselves or to resolve their thoughts into some meaningful, cleansing action. So much introversion is not only harrowing; it can also be boring, particularly when carried on to the enormous lengths in which it appears in "Matthias at the Door" and "Avon's Harvest."

And yet with these strictures, the case against Robinson's poetry has pretty much been stated, and we have on our hands what remains after they have been acknowledged.

No poet ever understood loneliness or separateness better than Robinson or knew the self-consuming furnace that the brain can become in isolation, the suicidal hellishness of it, doomed as it is to feed on itself in answerless frustration, fated to this condition by the accident of human birth, which carries with it the hunger for certainty and the intolerable load of personal recollections. He understood loneliness in all its many forms and depths and was thus less interested in its conventional poetic aspects than he was in the loneliness of the man in the crowd, or alone with his thoughts of the dead, or feeling at some unforseen time the metaphysical loneliness, the *angst,* of being "lost among the stars," or becoming aware of the solitude that resides in comfort and in the affection of friend and family—that desperation at the heart of what is called happiness. It is only the poet and those involved who realize the inevitability and the despair of these situations, "Although, to the serene outsider,/There still would seem to be a way."

The acceptance of the fact that there is no way, that there is nothing to do about the sadness of most human beings when they are alone or speaking to others as if to themselves, that there is nothing to offer them but recognition, sympathy, compassion, deepens Robinson's best poems until we sense in them something other than art. A thing inside us is likely to shift from where it was, and our world view to change, though perhaps only slightly, toward a darker, deeper perspective. Robinson has been called a laureate of failure and has even been accused (if that is the word) of making a cult and a virtue of failure, but that assessment is not quite accurate. His subject was "the slow tragedy of haunted men," those whose "eyes are lit with a wrong light," those who believe that some earthly occurrence in the past (and now forever impossible) could have made all the difference, that some person dead or otherwise beyond reach, some life unlived and now unlivable, could have been the answer to everything. But these longings were seen by Robinson to be the delusions necessary to sustain life, for human beings, though they can live without hope, cannot live believing that no hope ever could have existed. For this reason, many of the poems deal with the unlived life, the man kept by his own nature or by circumstance from "what might have been his," but there is always the ironic Robinsonian overtone that what might have been would not have been much better than what is—and, indeed, might well have been worse; the failure would only have had its development and setting altered somewhat, but not its pain or its inevitability.

Though Robinson's dramatic sense was powerful and often profound, his narrative·sense was not. His narrative devices are few, and they are used again and again. The poet is always, for example, running into somebody in the street whom he knew under other circumstances and who is now a bum, a "slowly-freezing Santa Claus," a street-corner revivalist, or something equally comical-pathetic and cut off. The story of the person's passing from his former state to this one then becomes the poem, sometimes told by the derelict, the "ruin who meant well," and sometimes puzzled out by the poet himself, either with his deep, painful probing or, as in some of the later long poems, such as "The Man Who Died Twice," with an intolerable amount of poetical hemming and hawing, backing and filling.

And yet Robinson's peculiar elliptical vision, even when it is boring, is worth the reader's time. The tone of his voice is so distinctive, his technique so varied and resourceful, and his compassion so intense that something valuable comes through even the most wasteful of his productions. Not nearly enough has been made of Robinson's skill, the chief thing about which is that it is able to create, through an astonishing number of forms and subjects, the tone of a single voice, achieving variety within a tonal unity. And it is largely in this tone, the product of outlook (or, if I may be forgiven, inlook), technique, and personality, that Robinson's particular excellence lies; thus the tone is worth examining.

Robinson's mind was not sensuously rich, if by that is meant a Keatsian or Hopkinsian outgoingness into nature as a bodily experience and the trust and delight in nature that this attitude implies. His poetic interests are psychological and philosophical; he examines the splits between what is and what might have been, what must be and what cannot be. That Robinson sees these differences to matter very little, finally, does not mean that they do not matter to the people who suffer from them; it is, in fact, in this realm of delusionary and obsessive suffering that Robinson's poems take place. Though his mind was not rich in a sensuous way, it was both powerful and hesitant, as though suspended between strong magnets. This gives his work an unparalleled sensitivity in balance; and from this balance, this desperately poised uncertainty, emanates a compassion both very personal and cosmic—a compassion that one might well see as a substitute for the compassion that God failed to supply. It is ironic at times, it is bitter and self-mocking, but it is always compassion unalloyed by sentimentality; it has been earned, as it is the burden of the poems themselves to show. This attitude, this tone, runs from gentle, rueful humor—though based, even so, on stark constants of human fate such as the aging process and death—to the most terrible hopelessness. It may appear in the tortuous working out of a long passage, or it may gleam forth for an instant in surroundings not seen until its appearance to be frightening, as in the poem below.

"Isaac and Archibald" is a New England pastoral in which a twelve-year-old boy takes a long walk with an old man, Isaac, to visit another old man at his farm. Nothing much happens, except that both Isaac and Archibald manage to reveal to the boy the signs of mental decline and approaching death in the other. The two men drink cider; the boy sits and reflects, prefiguring as he does the mature man and poet he will become. The boy's awareness of death is built up by small, affectionate touches, some of them so swift and light that they are almost sure to be passed over by the hurried reader.

> Hardly had we turned in from the main road
> When Archibald, with one hand on his back
> And the other clutching his huge-headed cane,
> Came limping down to meet us.—"Well! well! well!"
> Said he; and then he looked at my red face,
> All streaked with dust and sweat, and shook my hand,
> And said it must have been a right smart walk
> That we had had that day from Tilbury Town.—
> "Magnificent," said Isaac; and he told
> About the beautiful west wind there was
> Which cooled and clarified the atmosphere.
> "You must have made it with your legs, I guess,"
> Said Archibald; and Isaac humored him

With one of those infrequent smiles of his
Which he kept in reserve, apparently,
For Archibald alone. "But why," said he,
"Should Providence have cider in the world
If not for such an afternoon as this?"
And Archibald, with a soft light in his eyes,
Replied that if he chose to go down cellar,
There he would find eight barrels—one of which
Was newly tapped, he said, and to his taste
An honor to the fruit. Isaac approved
Most heartily of that, and guided us
Forthwith, as if his venerable feet
Were measuring the turf in his own door-yard,
Straight to the open rollway. Down we went,
Out of the fiery sunshine to the gloom,
Grateful and half sepulchral, where we found
The barrels, like eight potent sentinels,
Close ranged along the wall. From one of them
A bright pine spile stuck out alluringly,
And on the black flat stone, just under it,
Glimmered a late-spilled proof that Archibald
Had spoken from unfeigned experience.
There was a fluted antique water-glass
Close by, and in it, prisoned, or at rest,
There was a cricket, of the soft brown sort
That feeds on darkness. Isaac turned him out,
And touched him with his thumb to make him jump . . .

Until the introduction of the cricket and the few words that
typify it, there is nothing startling in the passage, though it is quite
good Robinson, with the judicious adverb "alluringly" attached to the
protrusion of the pine spile and the lovely affectionate irony of
Archibald's "unfeigned experience" with the cider. But the cricket,
of the *sort* that feeds on darkness, changes the poem and brings it
into the central Robinsonian orbit. Here, the insect is a more terrify-
ing and mysterious creature—a better symbol for the context—than a
maggot or dead louse would be, for it is normally a benign spirit of
household and hearth. This simple way of referring to it, as though
the supposition that it "feeds on darkness" were the most obvious
and natural thing in the world to say about it, produces a haunting
effect when encountered along with the gentle old farmers' prox-
imity to death and the boy's budding awareness of it.

It may be inferred from the above passages that Robinson is not
a writer of unremitting brilliance or a master of the more obvious
technical virtuosities. He is, rather, as has been said, a poet of

quick, tangential thrusts, of sallies and withdrawals, of fleeting hints and glimpsed implications. In his longer poems, particularly, the impacts build up slowly, and it is only to those who have not the sensitivity to catch the sudden, baffling, half-revealing gleams—those who are "annoyed by no such evil whim/As death, or time, or truth"—that Robinson's poems are heavy and dull. Though he has a way, particularly in the later poems, of burying his glints of meaning pretty deeply in the material that makes them possible, Robinson at his best manages to use the massiveness of discourse and the swift, elusive gleam of illumination—the momentary flashing into the open of a stark, tragic hint, a fleeting generalization—as complementaries. And when the balance between these elements is right, the effect is unforgettable.

At times it appears that Robinson not only did not seek to avoid dullness but courted it and actually used it as a device, setting up his major points by means of it and making them doubly effective by contrast, without in the least violating the unity of tone or the huge, heavy drift of the poem toward its conclusion. He is a slow and patient poet; taking his time to say a thing as he wishes to say it is one of his fundamental qualities. This has worked against him, particularly since his work has survived into an age of anything but slow and patient readers. The pedestrian movement of much of his work has made him unpopular in an era when the piling on of startling effects, the cramming of the poetic line with all the spoils it can carry, is regarded not so much as a criterion of good or superior verse of a certain kind, but as poetry itself, other kinds being relegated to inferior categories yet to be defined. But Robinson's considered, unhurried lines, as uncomplicated in syntax as they are difficult in thought, in reality are, by virtue of their enormous sincerity, conviction, and quiet originality, a constant rebuke to those who conceive of poetry as verbal legerdemain or as the "superior amusement" that the late T. S. Eliot would have had it be.

The Robinson line is simple in the way that straightforward English prose is simple; the declarative sentence is made to do most of the work. His questions, though comparatively rare, are weighted with the agony of concern, involvement, and uncertainty. It is the thought, rather than the expression of the thought, that makes some of Robinson difficult, for he was almost always at pains to write simply, and his skills were everywhere subservient to this ideal. My personal favorite of Robinson's effects is his extremely subtle use of the line as a means of changing the meaning of the sentence that forms the line, the whole poem changing direction slightly but unmistakably with each such shift.

> What is it in me that you like so much,
> And love so little?

And yet for all his skill, Robinson's technical equipment is never obvious or obtrusive, as Hopkins', say, is. This is, of course, a tribute to his resourcefulness, for in his best pieces the manner of the poem is absorbed into its matter, and we focus not on the mode of saying but on the situations and characters into whose presence we have come.

IV

Robinson's favorite words, because they embody his favorite way of getting at any subject, are "may" and "might." The whole of the once-celebrated "The Man Against the Sky," for example, is built upon their use. When the poet sees a man climbing Mount Monadnock, it is, for the purposes of his poem, important that he *not* know who the man is or what he is doing there, so that the poem can string together a long series of conjectural possibilties as to who he might be, what might happen to him, and what he might conceivably represent.

> Even he, who stood where I had found him,
> On high with fire all round him,
> Who moved along the molten west,
> And over the round hill's crest
> That seemed half ready with him to go down,
> Flame-bitten and flame-cleft,
> As if there were to be no last thing left
> Of a nameless unimaginable town—
> Even he who climbed and vanished may have taken
> Down to the perils of a depth not known . . .

When he reaches the words "may have," the reader is in true Robinson country; he lives among alternatives, possibilties, doubts, and delusionary gleams of hope. This particular poem, which not only uses this approach but virtually hounds it to death, is not successful mainly because Robinson insists on being overtly philosophical and, at the end, on committing himself to a final view. Another shortcoming is that he is not sufficiently close to the man, for his poems are much better when he knows *something* of the circumstances of a human life, tells what he knows, and *then* speculates, for the unresolved quality of his ratiocinations, coupled with the usually terrible *facts*, enables him to make powerful and haunting use of conjecture and of his typical "may have" or "might not have" presentations of alternative possibilities.

It is also true of this poem that it has very little of the leavening of Robinson's irony, and this lack is detrimental to it. This irony has been widely commented upon, but not, I think, quite as accurately as it might have been. Though it infrequently has the appearance of callousness or even cruelty, a closer examination, a more receptive *feeling* of its effect, will usually show that it is neither. It is, rather, a product of a detachment based on helplessness, on the saving grace of humor that is called into play because nothing practical can be done and because the spectator of tragedy must find some way in which to save himself emotionally from the effects of what he has witnessed.

> No, no—forget your Cricket and your Ant,
> For I shall never set my name to theirs
> That now bespeak the very sons and heirs
> Incarnate of Queen Gossip and King Cant.
> The case of Leffingwell is mixed, I grant,
> And futile seems the burden that he bears;
> But are we sounding his forlorn affairs
> Who brand him parasite and sycophant?
>
> I tell you, Leffingwell was more than these;
> And if he prove a rather sorry knight,
> What quiverings in the distance of what light
> May not have lured him with high promises,
> And then gone down?—He may have been deceived;
> He may have lied—he did; and he believed.

The irony here is not based on showing in what ridiculous and humiliating ways the self-delusion of Leffingwell made of him a parasite and sycophant; it works through and past these things to the much larger proposition that such delusion is necessary to life; that, in fact, it is the condition that enables us to function at all. The manufacture and protection of the self-image is really the one constant, the one obsessive concern, of our existence. This idea was, of course, not new with Robinson, though it may be worth mentioning that many psychiatrists, among them Alfred Adler and Harry Stack Sullivan, place a primary emphasis on such interpretations of the human mentality. What should be noted is that the lies of Leffingwell and of Uncle Ananias are in their way truths, for they have in them that portion of the truth that comes not from fact but from the ideal.

> All summer long we loved him for the same
> Perennial inspiration of his lies . . .

There is something more here, something more positive, than there is in the gloomy and one-dimensional use of similar themes in, say, Eugene O'Neill's *The Iceman Cometh*, for in Robinson's poems the necessity to lie (and, with luck, sublimely) is connected to the desire to remake the world by remaking that portion of it that is oneself. Robinson shows the relation between such lies and the realities they must struggle to stay alive among, and he shows them with the shrewdness and humor of a man who has told such lies to himself but sadly knows them for what they are. The reader is likely to smile at the absurdity—but also to be left with a new kind of admiration for certain human traits that he had theretofore believed pathetic or contemptible.

v

These, then, are Robinson's kinds of originality, of poetic value— all of them subtle and half-hidden, muffled and disturbing,, answering little but asking those questions that are unpardonable, unforgettable, and necessary.

It is curious and wonderful that this scholarly, intelligent, childlike, tormented New England stoic, "always hungry for the nameless," always putting in the reader's mouth "some word that hurts your tongue," useless for anything but his art, protected by hardier friends all his life, but enormously courageous and utterly dedicated (he once told Chard Powers Smith at the very end of his life, "I could never have done *anything* but write poetry"), should have brought off what in its quiet, searching, laborious way is one of the most remarkable accomplishments of modern poetry. Far from indulging, as his detractors have maintained, in a kind of poetical know-nothingism, he actually brought to poetry a new kind of approach, making of a refusal to pronounce definitively on his subjects a virtue and of speculation upon possibilities an instrument that allows an unparalleled fullness to his presentations, as well as endowing them with some of the mysteriousness, futility, and proneness to multiple interpretation that incidents and lives possess in the actual world.

Robinson's best poetry is exactly that kind of communication that "tells the more the more it is not told." In creating a body of major poetry with devices usually thought to be unfruitful for the creative act—irresolution, abstraction, conjecture, a dry, nearly imageless mode of address that tends always toward the general without ever supplying the resolving judgment that we expect of generalization —Robinson has done what good poets have always done: by means of his "cumulative silences" as well as by his actual lines, he has forced us to reexamine and finally to redefine what poetry is—or our notion of it—and so has enabled poetry itself to include more, to *be* more, than it was before he wrote.

March, 1965   JAMES DICKEY

SELECTED POEMS

of

Edwin Arlington Robinson

From

THE CHILDREN

OF THE NIGHT

1890–1897

———◆———

To

the Memory

of My Father

and Mother

DEAR FRIENDS

DEAR friends, reproach me not for what I do,
Nor counsel me, nor pity me; nor say
That I am wearing half my life away
For bubble-work that only fools pursue.
And if my bubbles be too small for you,
Blow bigger then your own: the games we play
To fill the frittered minutes of a day,
Good glasses are to read the spirit through.

And whoso reads may get him some shrewd skill;
And some unprofitable scorn resign,
To praise the very thing that he deplores;
So, friends (dear friends), remember, if you will,
The shame I win for singing is all mine,
The gold I miss for dreaming is all yours.

THE ALTAR

ALONE, remote, nor witting where I went,
I found an altar builded in a dream—
A fiery place, whereof there was a gleam
So swift, so searching, and so eloquent
Of upward promise, that love's murmur, blent
With sorrow's warning, gave but a supreme
Unending impulse to that human stream
Whose flood was all for the flame's fury bent.

Alas! I said,—the world is in the wrong.
But the same quenchless fever of unrest
That thrilled the foremost of that martyred throng
Thrilled me, and I awoke . . . and was the same
Bewildered insect plunging for the flame
That burns, and must burn somehow for the best.

3

JOHN EVERELDOWN

"WHERE are you going to-night, to-night,—
   Where are you going, John Evereldown?
There's never the sign of a star in sight,
   Nor a lamp that's nearer than Tilbury Town.
Why do you stare as a dead man might?
Where are you pointing away from the light?
And where are you going to-night, to-night,—
   Where are you going, John Evereldown?"

"Right through the forest, where none can see,
   There's where I'm going, to Tilbury Town.
The men are asleep,—or awake, may be,—
   But the women are calling John Evereldown.
Ever and ever they call for me,
And while they call can a man be free?
So right through the forest, where none can see,
   There's where I'm going, to Tilbury Town."

"But why are you going so late, so late,—
   Why are you going, John Evereldown?
Though the road be smooth and the way be straight,
   There are two long leagues to Tilbury Town.
Come in by the fire, old man, and wait!
Why do you chatter out there by the gate?
And why are you going so late, so late,—
   Why are you going, John Evereldown?"

"I follow the women wherever they call,—
   That's why I'm going to Tilbury Town.
God knows if I pray to be done with it all,
   But God is no friend to John Evereldown.
So the clouds may come and the rain may fall,
The shadows may creep and the dead men crawl,—
But I follow the women wherever they call,
   And that's why I'm going to Tilbury Town."

4

LUKE HAVERGAL

Go to the western gate, Luke Havergal,
There where the vines cling crimson on the wall,
And in the twilight wait for what will come.
The leaves will whisper there of her, and some,
Like flying words, will strike you as they fall;
But go, and if you listen she will call.
Go to the western gate, Luke Havergal—
Luke Havergal.

No, there is not a dawn in eastern skies
To rift the fiery night that's in your eyes;
But there, where western glooms are gathering,
The dark will end the dark, if anything:
God slays Himself with every leaf that flies,
And hell is more than half of paradise.
No, there is not a dawn in eastern skies—
In eastern skies.

Out of a grave I come to tell you this,
Out of a grave I come to quench the kiss
That flames upon your forehead with a glow
That blinds you to the way that you must go.
Yes, there is yet one way to where she is,
Bitter, but one that faith may never miss.
Out of a grave I come to tell you this—
To tell you this.

There is the western gate, Luke Havergal,
There are the crimson leaves upon the wall.
Go, for the winds are tearing them away,—
Nor think to riddle the dead words they say,
Nor any more to feel them as they fall;
But go, and if you trust her she will call.
There is the western gate, Luke Havergal—
Luke Havergal.

THREE QUATRAINS

I

As long as Fame's imperious music rings
    Will poets mock it with crowned words august;
And haggard men will clamber to be kings
    As long as Glory weighs itself in dust.

II

Drink to the splendor of the unfulfilled,
    Nor shudder for the revels that are done:
The wines that flushed Lucullus are all spilled,
    The strings that Nero fingered are all gone.

III

We canot crown ourselves with everything,
    Nor can we coax the Fates for us to quarrel:
No matter what we are, or what we sing,
    Time finds a withered leaf in every laurel.

AN OLD STORY

STRANGE that I did not know him then,
    That friend of mine!
I did not even show him then
    One friendly sign;

But cursed him for the ways he had
    To make me see
My envy of the praise he had
    For praising me.

I would have rid the earth of him
  Once, in my pride. . . .
I never knew the worth of him
  Until he died.

BALLADE OF BROKEN FLUTES

(*To A. T. Schumann*)

In dreams I crossed a barren land,
  A land of ruin, far away;
Around me hung on every hand
  A deathful stillness of decay;
  And silent, as in bleak dismay
That song should thus forsaken be,
  On that forgotten ground there lay
The broken flutes of Arcady.

The forest that was all so grand
  When pipes and tabors had their sway
Stood leafless now, a ghostly band
  Of skeletons in cold array.
  A lonely surge of ancient spray
Told of an unforgetful sea,
  But iron blows had hushed for aye
The broken flutes of Arcady.

No more by summer breezes fanned,
  The place was desolate and gray;
But still my dream was to command
  New life into that shrunken clay.
  I tried it. And you scan to-day,
With uncommiserating glee,
  The songs of one who strove to play
The broken flutes of Arcady.

So, Rock, I join the common fray,
    To fight where Mammon may decree;
And leave, to crumble as they may,
    The broken flutes of Arcady.

VILLANELLE OF CHANGE

SINCE Persia fell at Marathon,
    The yellow years have gathered fast:
Long centuries have come and gone.

And yet (they say) the place will don
    A phantom fury of the past,
Since Persia fell at Marathon;

And as of old, when Helicon
    Trembled and swayed with rapture vast
(Long centuries have come and gone),

This ancient plain, when night comes on,
    Shakes to a ghostly battle-blast,
Since Persia fell at Marathon.

But into soundless Acheron
    The glory of Greek shame was cast:
Long centuries have come and gone,

The suns of Hellas have all shone,
    The first has fallen to the last:—
Since Persia fell at Marathon,
Long centuries have come and gone.

THE HOUSE ON THE HILL

THEY are all gone away,
  The House is shut and still,
There is nothing more to say.

Through broken walls and gray
  The winds blow bleak and shrill:
They are all gone away.

Nor is there one to-day
  To speak them good or ill:
There is nothing more to say.

Why is it then we stray
  Around the sunken sill?
They are all gone away,

And our poor fancy-play
  For them is wasted skill:
There is nothing more to say.

There is ruin and decay
  In the House on the Hill:
They are all gone away,
There is nothing more to say.

RICHARD CORY

WHENEVER Richard Cory went down town,
We people on the pavement looked at him:
He was a gentleman from sole to crown,
Clean favored, and imperially slim.

9

And he was always quietly arrayed,
And he was always human when he talked;
But still he fluttered pulses when he said,
"Good-morning," and he glittered when he walked.

And he was rich—yes, richer than a king—
And admirably schooled in every grace:
In fine, we thought that he was everything
To make us wish that we were in his place.

So on we worked, and waited for the light,
And went without the meat, and cursed the bread;
And Richard Cory, one calm summer night,
Went home and put a bullet through his head.

BOSTON

My northern pines are good enough for me,
But there's a town my memory uprears—
A town that always like a friend appears,
And always in the sunrise by the sea.
And over it, somehow, there seems to be
A downward flash of something new and fierce,
That ever strives to clear, but never clears
The dimness of a charmed antiquity.

CALVARY

FRIENDLESS and faint, with martyred steps and slow,
Faint for the flesh, but for the spirit free,
Stung by the mob that came to see the show,
The Master toiled along to Calvary;

We gibed him, as he went, with houndish glee,
Till his dimmed eyes for us did overflow;
We cursed his vengeless hands thrice wretchedly,—
And this was nineteen hundred years ago.

But after nineteen hundred years the shame
Still clings, and we have not made good the loss
That outraged faith has entered in his name.
Ah, when shall come love's courage to be strong!
Tell me, O Lord—tell me, O Lord, how long
Are we to keep Christ writhing on the cross!

AMARYLLIS

ONCE, when I wandered in the woods alone,
An old man tottered up to me and said,
"Come, friend, and see the grave that I have made
For Amaryllis." There was in the tone
Of his complaint such quaver and such moan
That I took pity on him and obeyed,
And long stood looking where his hands had laid
An ancient woman, shrunk to skin and bone.

Far out beyond the forest I could hear
The calling of loud progress, and the bold
Incessant scream of commerce ringing clear;
But though the trumpets of the world were glad,
It made me lonely and it made me sad
To think that Amaryllis had grown old.

ZOLA

BECAUSE he puts the compromising chart
Of hell before your eyes, you are afraid;
Because he counts the price that you have paid
For innocence, and counts it from the start,
You loathe him. But he sees the human heart
Of God meanwhile, and in His hand was weighed
Your squeamish and emasculate crusade
Against the grim dominion of his art.

Never until we conquer the uncouth
Connivings of our shamed indifference
(We call it Christian faith) are we to scan
The racked and shrieking hideousness of Truth
To find, in hate's polluted self-defence
Throbbing, the pulse, the divine heart of man.

THE PITY OF THE LEAVES

VENGEFUL across the cold November moors,
Loud with ancestral shame there came the bleak
Sad wind that shrieked, and answered with a shriek
Reverberant through lonely corridors.
The old man heard it; and he heard, perforce,
Words out of lips that were no more to speak—
Words of the past that shook the old man's cheek
Like dead, remembered footsteps on old floors.

And then there were the leaves that plagued him so!
The brown, thin leaves that on the stones outside
Skipped with a freezing whisper. Now and then
They stopped, and stayed there—just to let him know
How dead they were, but if the old man cried,
They fluttered off like withered souls of men.

AARON STARK

WITHAL a meagre man was Aaron Stark,
Cursed and unkempt, shrewd, shrivelled, and morose.
A miser was he, with a miser's nose,
And eyes like little dollars in the dark.
His thin, pinched mouth was nothing but a mark;
And when he spoke there came like sullen blows
Through scattered fangs a few snarled words and close,
As if a cur were chary of its bark.

Glad for the murmur of his hard renown,
Year after year he shambled through the town,
A loveless exile moving with a staff;
And oftentimes there crept into his ears
A sound of alien pity, touched with tears,—
And then (and only then) did Aaron laugh.

CLIFF KLINGENHAGEN

CLIFF KLINGENHAGEN had me in to dine
With him one day; and after soup and meat,
And all the other things there were to eat,
Cliff took two glasses and filled one with wine
And one with wormwood. Then, without a sign
For me to choose at all, he took the draught
Of bitterness himself, and lightly quaffed
It off, and said the other one was mine.

And when I asked him what the deuce he meant
By doing that, he only looked at me
And smiled, and said it was a way of his.
And though I know the fellow, I have spent
Long time a-wondering when I shall be
As happy as Cliff Klingenhagen is.

THE DEAD VILLAGE

HERE there is death. But even here, they say,
Here where the dull sun shines this afternoon
As desolate as ever the dead moon
Did glimmer on dead Sardis, men were gay;
And there were little children here to play,
With small soft hands that once did keep in tune
The strings that stretch from heaven, till too soon
The change came, and the music passed away.

Now there is nothing but the ghosts of things,—
No life, no love, no children, and no men;
And over the forgotten place there clings
The strange and unrememberable light
That is in dreams. The music failed, and then
God frowned, and shut the village from His sight.

THE CLERKS

I DID not think that I should find them there
When I came back again; but there they stood,
As in the days they dreamed of when young blood
Was in their cheeks and women called them fair.
Be sure, they met me with an ancient air,—
And yes, there was a shop-worn brotherhood
About them; but the men were just as good,
And just as human as they ever were.

And you that ache so much to be sublime,
And you that feed yourselves with your descent,
What comes of all your visions and your fears?
Poets and kings are but the clerks of Time,
Tiering the same dull webs of discontent,
Clipping the same sad alnage of the years.

THOMAS HOOD

THE man who cloaked his bitterness within
This winding-sheet of puns and pleasantries,
God never gave to look with common eyes
Upon a world of anguish and of sin:
His brother was the branded man of Lynn;
And there are woven with his jollities
The nameless and eternal tragedies
That render hope and hopelessness akin.

We laugh, and crown him; but anon we feel
A still chord sorrow-swept,—a weird unrest;
And thin dim shadows home to midnight steal,
As if the very ghost of mirth were dead—
As if the joys of time to dreams had fled,
Or sailed away with Ines to the West.

HORACE TO LEUCONOË

I PRAY you not, Leuconoë, to pore
With unpermitted eyes on what may be
Appointed by the gods for you and me,
Nor on Chaldean figures any more.
'T were infinitely better to implore
The present only:—whether Jove decree
More winters yet to come, or whether he
Make even this, whose hard, wave-eaten shore
Shatters the Tuscan seas to-day, the last—
Be wise withal, and rack your wine, nor fill
Your bosom with large hopes; for while I sing,
The envious close of time is narrowing;—
So seize the day, or ever it be past,
And let the morrow come for what it will.

REUBEN BRIGHT

BECAUSE he was a butcher and thereby
Did earn an honest living (and did right),
I would not have you think that Reuben Bright
Was any more a brute than you or I;
For when they told him that his wife must die,
He stared at them, and shook with grief and fright,
And cried like a great baby half that night,
And made the women cry to see him cry.

And after she was dead, and he had paid
The singers and the sexton and the rest,
He packed a lot of things that she had made
Most mournfully away in an old chest
Of hers, and put some chopped-up cedar boughs
In with them, and tore down the slaughter-house.

THE TAVERN

WHENEVER I go by there nowadays
And look at the rank weeds and the strange grass,
The torn blue curtains and the broken glass,
I seem to be afraid of the old place;
And something stiffens up and down my face,
For all the world as if I saw the ghost
Of old Ham Amory, the murdered host,
With his dead eyes turned on me all aglaze.

The Tavern has a story, but no man
Can tell us what it is. We only know
That once long after midnight, years ago,
A stranger galloped up from Tilbury Town,
Who brushed, and scared, and all but overran
That skirt-crazed reprobate, John Evereldown.

GEORGE CRABBE

GIVE him the darkest inch your shelf allows,
Hide him in lonely garrets, if you will,—
But his hard, human pulse is throbbing still
With the sure strength that fearless truth endows.
In spite of all fine science disavows,
Of his plain excellence and stubborn skill
There yet remains what fashion cannot kill,
Though years have thinned the laurel from his brows.

Whether or not we read him, we can feel
From time to time the vigor of his name
Against us like a finger for the shame
And emptiness of what our souls reveal
In books that are as altars where we kneel
To consecrate the flicker, not the flame.

VERLAINE

WHY do you dig like long-clawed scavengers
To touch the covered corpse of him that fled
The uplands for the fens, and rioted
Like a sick satyr with doom's worshippers?
Come! let the grass grow there; and leave his verse
To tell the story of the life he led.
Let the man go: let the dead flesh be dead,
And let the worms be its biographers.

Song sloughs away the sin to find redress
In art's complete remembrance: nothing clings
For long but laurel to the stricken brow
That felt the Muse's finger; nothing less
Than hell's fulfilment of the end of things
Can blot the star that shines on Paris now.

SUPREMACY

THERE is a drear and lonely tract of hell
From all the common gloom removed afar:
A flat, sad land it is, where shadows are,
Whose lorn estate my verse may never tell.
I walked among them and I knew them well:
Men I had slandered on life's little star
For churls and sluggards; and I knew the scar
Upon their brows of woe ineffable.

But as I went majestic on my way,
Into the dark they vanished, one by one,
Till, with a shaft of God's eternal day,
The dream of all my glory was undone,—
And, with a fool's importunate dismay,
I heard the dead men singing in the sun.

THE TORRENT

I FOUND a torrent falling in a glen
Where the sun's light shone silvered and leaf-split;
The boom, the foam, and the mad flash of it
All made a magic symphony; but when
I thought upon the coming of hard men
To cut those patriarchal trees away,
And turn to gold the silver of that spray,
I shuddered. Yet a gladness now and then
Did wake me to myself till I was glad
In earnest, and was welcoming the time
For screaming saws to sound above the chime
Of idle waters, and for me to know
The jealous visionings that I had had
Were steps to the great place where trees and torrents go.

ON THE NIGHT OF A FRIEND'S WEDDING

If ever I am old, and all alone,
I shall have killed one grief, at any rate;
For then, thank God, I shall not have to wait
Much longer for the sheaves that I have sown.
The devil only knows what I have done,
But here I am, and here are six or eight
Good friends, who most ingenuously prate
About my songs to such and such a one.

But everything is all askew to-night,—
As if the time were come, or almost come,
For their untenanted mirage of me
To lose itself and crumble out of sight,
Like a tall ship that floats above the foam
A little while, and then breaks utterly.

L'ENVOI

Now in a thought, now in a shadowed word,
Now in a voice that thrills eternity,
Ever there comes an onward phrase to me
Of some transcendent music I have heard;
No piteous thing by soft hands dulcimered,
No trumpet crash of blood-sick victory,
But a glad strain of some vast harmony
That no brief mortal touch has ever stirred.

There is no music in the world like this,
No character wherewith to set it down,
No kind of instrument to make it sing.
No kind of instrument? Ah, yes, there is;
And after time and place are overthrown,
God's touch will keep its one chord quivering.

From

CAPTAIN CRAIG,

ETC.

1902

———◆◆———

To

the Memory

of John Hays

Gardiner

ISAAC AND ARCHIBALD

(To Mrs. Henry Richards)

Isaac and Archibald were two old men.
I knew them, and I may have laughed at them
A little; but I must have honored them
For they were old, and they were good to me.

I do not think of either of them now,
Without remembering, infallibly,
A journey that I made one afternoon
With Isaac to find out what Archibald
Was doing with his oats. It was high time
Those oats were cut, said Isaac; and he feared
That Archibald—well, he could never feel
Quite sure of Archibald. Accordingly
The good old man invited me—that is,
Permitted me—to go along with him;
And I, with a small boy's adhesiveness
To competent old age, got up and went.

I do not know that I cared overmuch
For Archibald's or anybody's oats,
But Archibald was quite another thing,
And Isaac yet another; and the world
Was wide, and there was gladness everywhere.
We walked together down the River Road
With all the warmth and wonder of the land
Around us, and the wayside flash of leaves,—
And Isaac said the day was glorious;
But somewhere at the end of the first mile
I found that I was figuring to find
How long those ancient legs of his would keep
The pace that he had set for them. The sun
Was hot, and I was ready to sweat blood;
But Isaac, for aught I could make of him,
Was cool to his hat-band. So I said then

With a dry gasp of affable despair,
Something about the scorching days we have
In August without knowing it sometimes;
But Isaac said the day was like a dream,
And praised the Lord, and talked about the breeze.
I made a fair confession of the breeze,
And crowded casually on his thought
The nearness of a profitable nook
That I could see. First I was half inclined
To caution him that he was growing old,
But something that was not compassion soon
Made plain the folly of all subterfuge.
Isaac was old, but not so old as that.

So I proposed, without an overture,
That we be seated in the shade a while,
And Isaac made no murmur. Soon the talk
Was turned on Archibald, and I began
To feel some premonitions of a kind
That only childhood knows; for the old man
Had looked at me and clutched me with his eye,
And asked if I had ever noticed things.
I told him that I could not think of them,
And I knew then, by the frown that left his face
Unsatisfied, that I had injured him.
"My good young friend," he said, "you cannot feel
What I have seen so long. You have the eyes—
Oh, yes—but you have not the other things:
The sight within that never will deceive,
You do not know—you have no right to know;
The twilight warning of experience,
The singular idea of loneliness,—
These are not yours. But they have long been mine,
And they have shown me now for seven years
That Archibald is changing. It is not
So much that he should come to his last hand,
And leave the game, and go the old way down;
But I have known him in and out so long,

And I have seen so much of good in him
That other men have shared and have not seen,
And I have gone so far through thick and thin,
Through cold and fire with him, that now it brings
To this old heart of mine an ache that you
Have not yet lived enough to know about.
But even unto you, and your boy's faith,
Your freedom, and your untried confidence,
A time will come to find out what it means
To know that you are losing what was yours,
To know that you are being left behind;
And then the long contempt of innocence—
God bless you, boy!—don't think the worse of it
Because an old man chatters in the shade—
Will all be like a story you have read
In childhood and remembered for the pictures.

And when the best friend of your life goes down,
When first you know in him the slackening
That comes, and coming always tells the end,—
Now in a common word that would have passed
Uncaught from any other lips than his,
Now in some trivial act of every day,
Done as he might have done it all along
But for a twinging little difference
That nips you like a squirrel's teeth—oh, yes,
Then you will understand it well enough.
But oftener it comes in other ways;
It comes without your knowing when it comes;
You know that he is changing, and you know
That he is going—just as I know now
That Archibald is going, and that I
Am staying. . . . Look at me, my boy,
And when the time shall come for you to see
That I must follow after him, try then
To think of me, to bring me back again,
Just as I was to-day. Think of the place
Where we are sitting now, and think of me—

Think of old Isaac as you knew him then,
When you set out with him in August once
To see old Archibald."—The words come back
Almost as Isaac must have uttered them,
And there comes with them a dry memory
Of something in my throat that would not move.

If you had asked me then to tell just why
I made so much of Isaac and the things
He said, I should have gone far for an answer;
For I knew it was not sorrow that I felt,
Whatever I may have wished it, or tried then
To make myself believe. My mouth was full
Of words, and they would have been comforting
To Isaac, spite of my twelve years, I think;
But there was not in me the willingness
To speak them out. Therefore I watched the ground;
And I was wondering what made the Lord
Create a thing so nervous as an ant,
When Isaac, with commendable unrest,
Ordained that we should take the road again—
For it was yet three miles to Archibald's,
And one to the first pump. I felt relieved
All over when the old man told me that;
I felt that he had stilled a fear of mine
That those extremities of heat and cold
Which he had long gone through with Archibald
Had made the man impervious to both;
But Isaac had a desert somewhere in him,
And at the pump he thanked God for all things
That He had put on earth for men to drink,
And he drank well,—so well that I proposed
That we go slowly lest I learn too soon
The bitterness of being left behind,
And all those other things. That was a joke
To Isaac, and it pleased him very much;
And that pleased me—for I was twelve years old.

At the end of an hour's walking after that
The cottage of old Archibald appeared.
Little and white and high on a smooth round hill
It stood, with hackmatacks and apple-trees
Before it, and a big barn-roof beyond;
And over the place—trees, houses, fields and all—
Hovered an air of still simplicity
And a fragrance of old summers—the old style
That lives the while it passes. I dare say
That I was lightly conscious of all this
When Isaac, of a sudden, stopped himself,
And for the long first quarter of a minute
Gazed with incredulous eyes, forgetful quite
Of breezes and of me and of all else
Under the scorching sun but a smooth-cut field,
Faint yellow in the distance. I was young,
But there were a few things that I could see,
And this was one of them.—"Well, well!" said he;
And "Archibald will be surprised, I think,"
Said I. But all my childhood subtlety
Was lost on Isaac, for he strode along
Like something out of Homer—powerful
And awful on the wayside, so I thought.
Also I thought how good it was to be
So near the end of my short-legged endeavor
To keep the pace with Isaac for five miles.

Hardly had we turned in from the main road
When Archibald, with one hand on his back
And the other clutching his huge-headed cane,
Came limping down to meet us.—"Well! well! well!"
Said he; and then he looked at my red face,
All streaked with dust and sweat, and shook my hand,
And said it must have been a right smart walk
That we had had that day from Tilbury Town.—
"Magnificent," said Isaac; and he told
About the beautiful west wind there was

Which cooled and clarified the atmosphere.
"You must have made it with your legs, I guess,"
Said Archibald; and Isaac humored him
With one of those infrequent smiles of his
Which he kept in reserve, apparently,
For Archibald alone. "But why," said he,
"Should Providence have cider in the world
If not for such an afternoon as this?"
And Archibald, with a soft light in his eyes,
Replied that if he chose to go down cellar,
There he would find eight barrels—one of which
Was newly tapped, he said, and to his taste
An honor to the fruit. Isaac approved
Most heartily of that, and guided us
Forthwith, as if his venerable feet
Were measuring the turf in his own door-yard,
Straight to the open rollway. Down we went,
Out of the fiery sunshine to the gloom,
Grateful and half sepulchral, where we found
The barrels, like eight potent sentinels,
Close ranged along the wall. From one of them
A bright pine spile stuck out alluringly,
And on the black flat stone, just under it,
Glimmered a late-spilled proof that Archibald
Had spoken from unfeigned experience.
There was a fluted antique water-glass
Close by, and in it, prisoned, or at rest,
There was a cricket, of the brown soft sort
That feeds on darkness. Isaac turned him out,
And touched him with his thumb to make him jump,
And then composedly pulled out the plug
With such a practised hand that scarce a drop
Did even touch his fingers. Then he drank
And smacked his lips with a slow patronage
And looked along the line of barrels there
With a pride that may have been forgetfulness
That they were Archibald's and not his own.
"I never twist a spigot nowadays,"

He said, and raised the glass up to the light,
"But I thank God for orchards." And that glass
Was filled repeatedly for the same hand
Before I thought it worth while to discern
Again that I was young, and that old age,
With all his woes, had some advantages.

"Now, Archibald," said Isaac, when we stood
Outside again, "I have it in my mind
That I shall take a sort of little walk—
To stretch my legs and see what you are doing.
You stay and rest your back and tell the boy
A story: Tell him all about the time
In Stafford's cabin forty years ago,
When four of us were snowed up for ten days
With only one dried haddock. Tell him all
About it, and be wary of your back.
Now I will go along."—I looked up then
At Archibald, and as I looked I saw
Just how his nostrils widened once or twice
And then grew narrow. I can hear to-day
The way the old man chuckled to himself—
Not wholesomely, not wholly to convince
Another of his mirth,—as I can hear
The lonely sigh that followed.—But at length
He said: "The orchard now's the place for us;
We may find something like an apple there,
And we shall have the shade, at any rate."
So there we went and there we laid ourselves
Where the sun could not reach us; and I champed
A dozen of worm-blighted astrakhans
While Archibald said nothing—merely told
The tale of Stafford's cabin, which was good,
Though "master chilly"—after his own phrase—
Even for a day like that. But other thoughts
Were moving in his mind, imperative,
And writhing to be spoken: I could see
The glimmer of them in a glance or two,

29

Cautious, or else unconscious, that he gave
Over his shoulder: . . . "Stafford and the rest—
But that's an old song now, and Archibald
And Isaac are old men. Remember, boy,
That we are old. Whatever we have gained,
Or lost, or thrown away, we are old men.
You look before you and we look behind,
And we are playing life out in the shadow—
But that's not all of it. The sunshine lights
A good road yet before us if we look,
And we are doing that when least we know it;
For both of us are children of the sun,
Like you, and like the weed there at your feet.
The shadow calls us, and it frightens us—
We think; but there's a light behind the stars
And we old fellows who have dared to live,
We see it—and we see the other things,
The other things . . . Yes, I have seen it come
These eight years, and these ten years, and I know
Now that it cannot be for very long
That Isaac will be Isaac. You have seen—
Young as you are, you must have seen the strange
Uncomfortable habit of the man?
He'll take my nerves and tie them in a knot
Sometimes, and that's not Isaac. I know that—
And I know what it is: I get it here
A little, in my knees, and Isaac—here."
The old man shook his head regretfully
And laid his knuckles three times on his forehead.
"That's what it is: Isaac is not quite right.
You see it, but you don't know what it means:
The thousand little differences—no,
You do not know them, and it's well you don't;
You'll know them soon enough—God bless you, boy!—
You'll know them, but not all of them—not all.
So think of them as little as you can:
There's nothing in them for you, or for me—
But I am old and I must think of them;

I'm in the shadow, but I don't forget
The light, my boy,—the light behind the stars.
Remember that: remember that I said it;
And when the time that you think far away
Shall come for you to say it—say it, boy;
Let there be no confusion or distrust
In you, no snarling of a life half lived,
Nor any cursing over broken things
That your complaint has been the ruin of.
Live to see clearly and the light will come
To you, and as you need it.—But there, there,
I'm going it again, as Isaac says,
And I'll stop now before you go to sleep.—
Only be sure that you growl cautiously,
And always where the shadow may not reach you."

Never shall I forget, long as I live,
The quaint thin crack in Archibald's voice,
The lonely twinkle in his little eyes,
Or the way it made me feel to be with him.
I know I lay and looked for a long time
Down through the orchard and across the road,
Across the river and the sun-scorched hills
That ceased in a blue forest, where the world
Ceased with it. Now and then my fancy caught
A flying glimpse of a good life beyond—
Something of ships and sunlight, streets and singing,
Troy falling, and the ages coming back,
And ages coming forward: Archibald
And Isaac were good fellows in old clothes,
And Agamemnon was a friend of mine;
Ulysses coming home again to shoot
With bows and feathered arrows made another,
And all was as it should be. I was young.

So I lay dreaming of what things I would,
Calm and incorrigibly satisfied
With apples and romance and ignorance,

And the still smoke from Archibald's clay pipe.
There was a stillness over everything,
As if the spirit of heat had laid its hand
Upon the world and hushed it; and I felt
Within the mightiness of the white sun
That smote the land around us and wrought out
A fragrance from the trees, a vital warmth
And fullness for the time that was to come,
And a glory for the world beyond the forest.
The present and the future and the past,
Isaac and Archibald, the burning bush,
The Trojans and the walls of Jericho,
Were beautifully fused; and all went well
Till Archibald began to fret for Isaac
And said it was a master day for sunstroke.
That was enough to make a mummy smile,
I thought; and I remained hilarious,
In face of all precedence and respect,
Till Isaac (who had come to us unheard)
Found he had no tobacco, looked at me
Peculiarly, and asked of Archibald
What ailed the boy to make him chirrup so.
From that he told us what a blessed world
The Lord had given us.—"But, Archibald,"
He added, with a sweet severity
That made me think of peach-skins and goose-flesh,
"I'm half afraid you cut those oats of yours
A day or two before they were well set."
"They were set well enough," said Archibald,—
And I remarked the process of his nose
Before the words came out. "But never mind
Your neighbor's oats: you stay here in the shade
And rest yourself while I go find the cards.
We'll have a little game of seven-up
And let the boy keep count."—"We'll have the game,
Assuredly," said Isaac; "and I think
That I will have a drop of cider, also."

They marched away together towards the house
And left me to my childish ruminations
Upon the ways of men. I followed them
Down cellar with my fancy, and then left them
For a fairer vision of all things at once
That was anon to be destroyed again
By the sound of voices and of heavy feet—
One of the sounds of life that I remember,
Though I forget so many that rang first
As if they were thrown down to me from Sinai.

So I remember, even to this day,
Just how they sounded, how they placed themselves,
And how the game went on while I made marks
And crossed them out, and meanwhile made some Trojans.
Likewise I made Ulysses, after Isaac,
And a little after Flaxman. Archibald
Was injured when he found himself left out,
But he had no heroics, and I said so:
I told him that his white beard was too long
And too straight down to be like things in Homer.
"Quite so," said Isaac.—"Low," said Archibald;
And he threw down a deuce with a deep grin
That showed his yellow teeth and made me happy.
So they played on till a bell rang from the door,
And Archibald said, "Supper."—After that
The old men smoked while I sat watching them
And wondered with all comfort what might come
To me, and what might never come to me;
And when the time came for the long walk home
With Isaac in the twilight, I could see
The forest and the sunset and the sky-line,
No matter where it was that I was looking:
The flame beyond the boundary, the music,
The foam and the white ships, and two old men
Were things that would not leave me.—And that night
There came to me a dream—a shining one,

With two old angels in it. They had wings,
And they were sitting where a silver light
Suffused them, face to face. The wings of one
Began to palpitate as I approached,
But I was yet unseen when a dry voice
Cried thinly, with unpatronizing triumph,
"I've got you, Isaac; high, low, jack, and the game."

Isaac and Archibald have gone their way
To the silence of the loved and well-forgotten.
I knew them, and I may have laughed at them;
But there's a laughing that has honor in it,
And I have no regret for light words now.
Rather I think sometimes they may have made
Their sport of me;—but they would not do that,
They were too old for that. They were old men,
And I may laugh at them because I knew them.

AUNT IMOGEN

AUNT IMOGEN was coming, and therefore
The children—Jane, Sylvester, and Young George—
Were eyes and ears; for there was only one
Aunt Imogen to them in the whole world,
And she was in it only for four weeks
In fifty-two. But those great bites of time
Made all September a Queen's Festival;
And they would strive, informally, to make
The most of them.—The mother understood,
And wisely stepped away. Aunt Imogen
Was there for only one month in the year,
While she, the mother,—she was always there;
And that was what made all the difference.
She knew it must be so, for Jane had once
Expounded it to her so learnedly

That she had looked away from the child's eyes
And thought; and she had thought of many things.

There was a demonstration every time
Aunt Imogen appeared, and there was more
Than one this time. And she was at a loss
Just how to name the meaning of it all:
It puzzled her to think that she could be
So much to any crazy thing alive—
Even to her sister's little savages
Who knew no better than to be themselves;
But in the midst of her glad wonderment
She found herself besieged and overcome
By two tight arms and one tumultuous head,
And therewith half bewildered and half pained
By the joy she felt and by the sudden love
That proved itself in childhood's honest noise.
Jane, by the wings of sex, had reached her first;
And while she strangled her, approvingly,
Sylvester thumped his drum and Young George howled.
But finally, when all was rectified,
And she had stilled the clamor of Young George
By giving him a long ride on her shoulders,
They went together into the old room
That looked across the fields; and Imogen
Gazed out with a girl's gladness in her eyes,
Happy to know that she was back once more
Where there were those who knew her, and at last
Had gloriously got away again
From cabs and clattered asphalt for a while;
And there she sat and talked and looked and laughed
And made the mother and the children laugh.
Aunt Imogen made everybody laugh.

There was the feminine paradox—that she
Who had so little sunshine for herself
Should have so much for others. How it was
That she could make, and feel for making it,

So much of joy for them, and all along
Be covering, like a scar, and while she smiled,
That hungering incompleteness and regret—
That passionate ache for something of her own,
For something of herself—she never knew.
She knew that she could seem to make them all
Believe there was no other part of her
Than her persistent happiness; but the why
And how she did not know. Still none of them
Could have a thought that she was living down—
Almost as if regret were criminal,
So proud it was and yet so profitless—
The penance of a dream, and that was good.
Her sister Jane—the mother of little Jane,
Sylvester, and Young George—might make herself
Believe she knew, for she—well, she was Jane.

Young George, however, did not yield himself
To nourish the false hunger of a ghost
That made no good return. He saw too much:
The accumulated wisdom of his years
Had so conclusively made plain to him
The permanent profusion of a world
Where everybody might have everything
To do, and almost everything to eat,
That he was jubilantly satisfied
And all unthwarted by adversity.
Young George knew things. The world, he had found out,
Was a good place, and life was a good game—
Particularly when Aunt Imogen
Was in it. And one day it came to pass—
One rainy day when she was holding him
And rocking him—that he, in his own right,
Took it upon himself to tell her so;
And something in his way of telling it—
The language, or the tone, or something else—
Gripped like insidious fingers on her throat,
And then went foraging as if to make

A plaything of her heart. Such undeserved
And unsophisticated confidence
Went mercilessly home; and had she sat
Before a looking glass, the deeps of it
Could not have shown more clearly to her then
Than one thought-mirrored little glimpse had shown
The pang that wrenched her face and filled her eyes
With anguish and intolerable mist.
The blow that she had vaguely thrust aside
Like fright so many times had found her now:
Clean-thrust and final it had come to her
From a child's lips at last, as it had come
Never before, and as it might be felt
Never again. Some grief, like some delight,
Stings hard but once: to custom after that
The rapture or the pain submits itself,
And we are wiser than we were before.
And Imogen was wiser; though at first
Her dream-defeating wisdom was indeed
A thankless heritage: there was no sweet,
No bitter now; nor was there anything
To make a daily meaning for her life—
Till truth, like Harlequin, leapt out somehow
From ambush and threw sudden savor to it—
But the blank taste of time. There were no dreams,
No phantoms in her future any more:
One clinching revelation of what was
One by-flash of irrevocable chance,
Had acridly but honestly foretold
The mystical fulfilment of a life
That might have once . . . But that was all gone by:
There was no need of reaching back for that:
The triumph was not hers: there was no love
Save borrowed love: there was no might have been.

But there was yet Young George—and he had gone
Conveniently to sleep, like a good boy;
And there was yet Sylvester with his drum,

37

And there was frowzle-headed little Jane;
And there was Jane the sister, and the mother,—
Her sister, and the mother of them all.
They were not hers, not even one of them:
She was not born to be so much as that,
For she was born to be Aunt Imogen.
Now she could see the truth and look at it;
Now she could make stars out where once had palled
A future's emptiness; now she could share
With others—ah, the others!—to the end
The largess of a woman who could smile;
Now it was hers to dance the folly down,
And all the murmuring; now it was hers
To be Aunt Imogen.—So, when Young George
Woke up and blinked at her with his big eyes,
And smiled to see the way she blinked at him,
'T was only in old concord with the stars
That she took hold of him and held him close,
Close to herself, and crushed him till he laughed.

THE GROWTH OF "LORRAINE"

I

WHILE I stood listening, discreetly dumb,
Lorraine was having the last word with me:
"I know," she said, "I know it, but you see
Some creatures are born fortunate, and some
Are born to be found out and overcome,—
Born to be slaves, to let the rest go free;
And if I'm one of them (and I must be)
You may as well forget me and go home.

"You tell me not to say these things, I know,
But I should never try to be content:

I've gone too far; the life would be too slow.
Some could have done it—some girls have the stuff;
But I can't do it: I don't know enough.
I'm going to the devil."—And she went.

II

I DID not half believe her when she said
That I should never hear from her again;
Nor when I found a letter from Lorraine,
Was I surprised or grieved at what I read:
"Dear friend, when you find this, I shall be dead.
You are too far away to make me stop.
They say that one drop—think of it, one drop!—
Will be enough,—but I'll take five instead.

"You do not frown because I call you friend,
For I would have you glad that I still keep
Your memory, and even at the end—
Impenitent, sick, shattered—cannot curse
The love that flings, for better or for worse,
This worn-out, cast-out flesh of mine to sleep."

ERASMUS

WHEN he protested, not too solemnly,
That for a world's achieving maintenance
The crust of overdone divinity
Lacked aliment, they called it recreance;
And when he chose through his own glass to scan
Sick Europe, and reduced, unyieldingly,
The monk within the cassock to the man
Within the monk, they called it heresy.

And when he made so perilously bold
As to be scattered forth in black and white,

Good fathers looked askance at him and rolled
Their inward eyes in anguish and affright;
There were some of them did shake at what was told
And they shook best who knew that he was right.

THE BOOK OF ANNANDALE

I

PARTLY to think, more to be left alone,
George Annandale said something to his friends—
A word or two, brusque, but yet smoothed enough
To suit their funeral gaze—and went upstairs;
And there, in the one room that he could call
His own, he found a sort of meaningless
Annoyance in the mute familiar things
That filled it; for the grate's monotonous gleam
Was not the gleam that he had known before,
The books were not the books that used to be,
The place was not the place. There was a lack
Of something; and the certitude of death
Itself, as with a furtive questioning,
Hovered, and he could not yet understand.
He knew that she was gone—there was no need
Of any argued proof to tell him that,
For they had buried her that afternoon,
Under the leaves and snow; and still there was
A doubt, a pitiless doubt, a plunging doubt,
That struck him, and upstartled when it struck,
The vision, the old thought in him. There was
A lack, and one that wrenched him; but it was
Not that—not that. There was a present sense
Of something indeterminably near—
The soul-clutch of a prescient emptiness
That would not be foreboding. And if not,
What then?—or was it anything at all?

Yes, it was something—it was everything—
But what was everything? or anything?

Tired of time, bewildered, he sat down;
But in his chair he kept on wondering
That he should feel so desolately strange
And yet—for all he knew that he had lost
More of the world than most men ever win—
So curiously calm. And he was left
Unanswered and unsatisfied: there came
No clearer meaning to him than had come
Before; the old abstraction was the best
That he could find, the farthest he could go;
To that was no beginning and no end—
No end that he could reach. So he must learn
To live the surest and the largest life
Attainable in him, would he divine
The meaning of the dream and of the words
That he had written, without knowing why,
On sheets that he had bound up like a book
And covered with red leather. There it was—
There in his desk, the record he had made,
The spiritual plaything of his life:
There were the words no eyes had ever seen
Save his; there were the words that were not made
For glory or for gold. The pretty wife
Whom he had loved and lost had not so much
As heard of them. They were not made for her.
His love had been so much the life of her,
And hers had been so much the life of him,
That any wayward phrasing on his part
Would have had no moment. Neither had lived enough
To know the book, albeit one of them
Had grown enough to write it. There it was,
However, though he knew not why it was:
There was the book, but it was not for her,
For she was dead. And yet, there was the book.
Thus would his fancy circle out and out,

And out and in again, till he would make
As if with a large freedom to crush down
Those under-thoughts. He covered with his hands
His tired eyes, and waited: he could hear—
Or partly feel and hear, mechanically—
The sound of talk, with now and then the steps
And skirts of some one scudding on the stairs,
Forgetful of the nerveless funeral feet
That she had brought with her; and more than once
There came to him a call as of a voice—
A voice of love returning—but not hers.
Whose he knew not, nor dreamed; nor did he know,
Nor did he dream, in his blurred loneliness
Of thought, what all the rest might think of him.

For it had come at last, and she was gone
With all the vanished women of old time,—
And she was never coming back again.
Yes, they had buried her that afternoon,
Under the frozen leaves and the cold earth,
Under the leaves and snow. The flickering week,
The sharp and certain day, and the long drowse
Were over, and the man was left alone.
He knew the loss—therefore it puzzled him
That he should sit so long there as he did,
And bring the whole thing back—the love, the trust,
The pallor, the poor face, and the faint way
She last had looked at him—and yet not weep,
Or even choose to look about the room
To see how sad it was; and once or twice
He winked and pinched his eyes against the flame
And hoped there might be tears. But hope was all,
And all to him was nothing: he was lost.
And yet he was not lost: he was astray—
Out of his life and in another life;
And in the stillness of this other life
He wondered and he drowsed. He wondered when
It was, and wondered if it ever was

On earth that he had known the other face—
The searching face, the eloquent, strange face—
That with a sightless beauty looked at him
And with a speechless promise uttered words
That were not the world's words, or any kind
That he had known before. What was it, then?
What was it held him—fascinated him?
Why should he not be human? He could sigh,
And he could even groan,—but what of that?
There was no grief left in him. Was he glad?

Yet how could he be glad, or reconciled,
Or anything but wretched and undone?
How could he be so frigid and inert—
So like a man with water in his veins
Where blood had been a little while before?
How could he sit shut in there like a snail?
What ailed him? What was on him? Was he glad?
Over and over again the question came,
Unanswered and unchanged,—and there he was.
But what in heaven's name did it all mean?
If he had lived as other men had lived,
If home had ever shown itself to be
The counterfeit that others had called home,
Then to this undivined resource of his
There were some key; but now . . . Philosophy?
Yes, he could reason in a kind of way
That he was glad for Miriam's release—
Much as he might be glad to see his friends
Laid out around him with their grave-clothes on,
And this life done for them; but something else
There was that foundered reason, overwhelmed it,
And with a chilled, intuitive rebuff
Beat back the self-cajoling sophistries
That his half-tutored thought would half-project.

What was it, then? Had he become transformed
And hardened through long watches and long grief

Into a loveless, feelingless dead thing
That brooded like a man, breathed like a man,—
Did everything but ache? And was a day
To come some time when feeling should return
Forever to drive off that other face—
The lineless, indistinguishable face—
That once had thrilled itself between his own
And hers there on the pillow,—and again
Between him and the coffin-lid had flashed
Like fate before it closed,—and at the last
Had come, as it should seem, to stay with him,
Bidden or not? He were a stranger then,
Foredrowsed awhile by some deceiving draught
Of poppied anguish, to the covert grief
And the stark loneliness that waited him,
And for the time were cursedly endowed
With a dull trust that shammed indifference
To knowing there would be no touch again
Of her small hand on his, no silencing
Of her quick lips on his, no feminine
Completeness and love-fragrance in the house,
No sound of some one singing any more,
No smoothing of slow fingers on his hair,
No shimmer of pink slippers on brown tiles.

But there was nothing, nothing, in all that:
He had not fooled himself so much as that;
He might be dreaming or he might be sick,
But not like that. There was no place for fear,
No reason for remorse. There was the book
That he had made, though. . . . It might be the book;
Perhaps he might find something in the book;
But no, there could be nothing there at all—
He knew it word for word; but what it meant—
He was not sure that he had written it
For what it meant; and he was not quite sure
That he had written it;—more likely it
Was all a paper ghost. . . . But the dead wife

Was real: he knew all that, for he had been
To see them bury her; and he had seen
The flowers and the snow and the stripped limbs
Of trees; and he had heard the preacher pray;
And he was back again, and he was glad.
Was he a brute? No, he was not a brute:
He was a man—like any other man:
He had loved and married his wife Miriam,
They had lived a little while in paradise
And she was gone; and that was all of it.

But no, not all of it—not all of it:
There was the book again; something in that
Pursued him, overpowered him, put out
The futile strength of all his whys and wheres,
And left him unintelligibly numb—
Too numb to care for anything but rest.
It must have been a curious kind of book
That he had made it: it was a drowsy book
At any rate. The very thought of it
Was like the taste of some impossible drink—
A taste that had no taste, but for all that
Had mixed with it a strange thought-cordial,
So potent that it somehow killed in him
The ultimate need of doubting any more—
Of asking any more. Did he but live
The life that he must live, there were no more
To seek.—The rest of it was on the way.

Still there was nothing, nothing, in all this—
Nothing that he cared now to reconcile
With reason or with sorrow. All he knew
For certain was that he was tired out:
His flesh was heavy and his blood beat small;
Something supreme had been wrenched out of him
As if to make vague room for something else.
He had been through too much. Yes, he would stay
There where he was and rest.—And there he stayed;

The daylight became twilight, and he stayed;
The flame and the face faded, and he slept.
And they had buried her that afternoon,
Under the tight-screwed lid of a long box,
Under the earth, under the leaves and snow.

II

Look where she would, feed conscience how she might,
There was but one way now for Damaris—
One straight way that was hers, hers to defend,
At hand, imperious. But the nearness of it,
The flesh-bewildering simplicity,
And the plain strangeness of it, thrilled again
That wretched little quivering single string
Which yielded not, but held her to the place
Where now for five triumphant years had slept
The flameless dust of Argan.—He was gone,
The good man she had married long ago;
And she had lived, and living she had learned,
And surely there was nothing to regret:
Much happiness had been for each of them,
And they had been like lovers to the last:
And after that, and long, long after that,
Her tears had washed out more of widowed grief
Than smiles had ever told of other joy.—
But could she, looking back, find anything
That should return to her in the new time,
And with relentless magic uncreate
This temple of new love where she had thrown
Dead sorrow on the altar of new life?
Only one thing, only one thread was left;
When she broke that, when reason snapped it off,
And once for all, baffled, the grave let go
The trivial hideous hold it had on her,—
Then she were free, free to be what she would,
Free to be what she was.—And yet she stayed,
Leashed, as it were, and with a cobweb strand,
Close to a tombstone—maybe to starve there.

But why to starve? And why stay there at all?
Why not make one good leap and then be done
Forever and at once with Argan's ghost
And all such outworn churchyard servitude?
For it was Argan's ghost that held the string,
And her sick fancy that held Argan's ghost—
Held it and pitied it. She laughed, almost,
There for the moment; but her strained eyes filled
With tears, and she was angry for those tears—
Angry at first, then proud, then sorry for them.
So she grew calm; and after a vain chase
For thoughts more vain, she questioned of herself
What measure of primeval doubts and fears
Were still to be gone through that she might win
Persuasion of her strength and of herself
To be what she could see that she must be,
No matter where the ghost was.—And the more
She lived, the more she came to recognize
That something out of her thrilled ignorance
Was luminously, proudly being born,
And thereby proving, thought by forward thought,
The prowess of its image; and she learned
At length to look right on to the long days
Before her without fearing. She could watch
The coming course of them as if they were
No more than birds, that slowly, silently,
And irretrievably should wing themselves
Uncounted out of sight. And when he came
Again, she might be free—she would be free.
Else, when he looked at her she must look down,
Defeated, and malignly dispossessed
Of what was hers to prove and in the proving
Wisely to consecrate. And if the plague
Of that perverse defeat should come to be—
If at that sickening end she were to find
Herself to be the same poor prisoner
That he had found at first—then she must lose
All sight and sound of him, she must abjure

47

All possible thought of him; for he would go
So far and for so long from her that love—
Yes, even a love like his, exiled enough,
Might for another's touch be born again—
Born to be lost and starved for and not found;
Or, at the next, the second wretchedest,
It might go mutely flickering down and out,
And on some incomplete and piteous day,
Some perilous day to come, she might at last
Learn, with a noxious freedom, what it is
To be at peace with ghosts. Then were the blow
Thrice deadlier than any kind of death
Could ever be: to know that she had won
The truth too late—there were the dregs indeed
Of wisdom, and of love the final thrust
Unmerciful; and there where now did lie
So plain before her the straight radiance
Of what was her appointed way to take,
Were only the bleak ruts of an old road
That stretched ahead and faded and lay far
Through deserts of unconscionable years.

But vampire thoughts like these confessed the doubt
That love denied; and once, if never again,
They should be turned away. They might come back—
More craftily, perchance, they might come back—
And with a spirit-thirst insatiable
Finish the strength of her; but now, to-day
She would have none of them. She knew that love
Was true, that he was true, that she was true;
And should a death-bed snare that she had made
So long ago be stretched inexorably
Through all her life, only to be unspun
With her last breathing? And were bats and threads,
Accursedly devised with watered gules,
To be Love's heraldry? What were it worth
To live and to find out that life were life
But for an unrequited incubus

48

Of outlawed shame that would not be thrown down
Till she had thrown down fear and overcome
The woman that was yet so much of her
That she might yet go mad? What were it worth
To live, to linger, and to be condemned
In her submission to a common thought
That clogged itself and made of its first faith
Its last impediment? What augured it,
Now in this quick beginning of new life,
To clutch the sunlight and be feeling back,
Back with a scared fantastic fearfulness,
To touch, not knowing why, the vexed-up ghost
Of what was gone?

                    Yes, there was Argan's face,
Pallid and pinched and ruinously marked
With big pathetic bones; there were his eyes,
Quiet and large, fixed wistfully on hers;
And there, close-pressed again within her own,
Quivered his cold thin fingers. And, ah! yes,
There were the words, those dying words again,
And hers that answered when she promised him.
Promised him? . . . yes. And had she known the truth
Of what she felt that he should ask her that,
And had she known the love that was to be,
God knew that she could not have told him then.
But then she knew it not, nor thought of it;
There was no need of it; nor was there need
Of any problematical support
Whereto to cling while she convinced herself
That love's intuitive utility,
Inexorably merciful, had proved
That what was human was unpermanent
And what was flesh was ashes. She had told
Him then that she would love no other man,
That there was not another man on earth
Whom she could ever love, or who could make
So much as a love thought go through her brain;

And he had smiled. And just before he died
His lips had made as if to say something—
Something that passed unwhispered with his breath,
Out of her reach, out of all quest of it.
And then, could she have known enough to know
The meaning of her grief, the folly of it,
The faithlessness and the proud anguish of it,
There might be now no threads to punish her,
No vampire thoughts to suck the coward blood,
The life, the very soul of her.

                                        Yes, Yes,
They might come back. . . . But why should they come back?
Why was it she had suffered? Why had she
Struggled and grown these years to demonstrate
That close without those hovering clouds of gloom
And through them here and there forever gleamed
The Light itself, the life, the love, the glory,
Which was of its own radiance good proof
That all the rest was darkness and blind sight?
And who was *she?* The woman she had known—
The woman she had petted and called "I"—
The woman she had pitied, and at last
Commiserated for the most abject
And persecuted of all womankind,—
Could it be she that had sought out the way
To measure and thereby to quench in her
The woman's fear—the fear of her not fearing?
A nervous little laugh that lost itself,
Like logic in a dream, fluttered her thoughts
An instant there that ever she should ask
What she might then have told so easily—
So easily that Annandale had frowned,
Had he been given wholly to be told
The truth of what had never been before
So passionately, so inevitably
Confessed.

For she could see from where she sat
The sheets that he had bound up like a book
And covered with red leather; and her eyes
Could see between the pages of the book,
Though her eyes, like them, were closed. And she could read
As well as if she had them in her hand,
What he had written on them long ago,—
Six years ago, when he was waiting for her.
She might as well have said that she could see
The man himself, as once he would have looked
Had she been there to watch him while he wrote
Those words, and all for her. . . . For her whose face
Had flashed itself, prophetic and unseen,
But not unspirited, between the life
That would have been without her and the life
That he had gathered up like frozen roots
Out of a grave-clod lying at his feet,
Unconsciously, and as unconsciously
Transplanted and revived. He did not know
The kind of life that he had found, nor did
He doubt, not knowing it; but well he knew
That it was life—new life, and that the old
Might then with unimprisoned wings go free,
Onward and all along to its own light,
Through the appointed shadow.

                                While she gazed
Upon it there she felt within herself
The growing of a newer consciousness—
The pride of something fairer than her first
Outclamoring of interdicted thought
Had ever quite foretold; and all at once
There quivered and requivered through her flesh,
Like music, like the sound of an old song,
Triumphant, love-remembered murmurings
Of what for passion's innocence had been
Too mightily, too perilously hers,

Ever to be reclaimed and realized
Until to-day. To-day she could throw off
The burden that had held her down so long,
And she could stand upright, and she could see
The way to take, with eyes that had in them
No gleam but of the spirit. Day or night,
No matter; she could see what was to see—
All that had been till now shut out from her,
The service, the fulfillment, and the truth,
And thus the cruel wiseness of it all.

So Damaris, more like than anything
To one long prisoned in a twilight cave
With hovering bats for all companionship,
And after time set free to fight the sun,
Laughed out, so glad she was to recognize
The test of what had been, through all her folly,
The courage of her conscience; for she knew,
Now on a late-flushed autumn afternoon
That else had been too bodeful of dead things
To be endured with aught but the same old
Inert, self-contradicted martyrdom
Which she had known so long, that she could look
Right forward through the years, nor any more
Shrink with a cringing prescience to behold
The glitter of dead summer on the grass,
Or the brown-glimmered crimson of still trees
Across the intervale where flashed along,
Black-silvered, the cold river. She had found,
As if by some transcendent freakishness
Of reason, the glad life that she had sought
Where naught but obvious clouds could ever be—
Clouds to put out the sunlight from her eyes,
And to put out the love-light from her soul.
But they were gone—now they were all gone;
And with a whimsied pathos, like the mist
Of grief that clings to new-found happiness
Hard wrought, she might have pity for the small

Defeated quest of them that brushed her sight
Like flying lint—lint that had once been thread. . . .

Yes, like an anodyne, the voice of him,
There were the words that he had made for her,
For her alone. The more she thought of them
The more she lived them, and the more she knew
The life-grip and the pulse of warm strength in them.
They were the first and last of words to her,
And there was in them a far questioning
That had for long been variously at work,
Divinely and elusively at work,
With her, and with the grave that had been hers;
They were eternal words, and they diffused
A flame of meaning that men's lexicons
Had never kindled; they were choral words
That harmonized with love's enduring chords
Like wisdom with release; triumphant words
That rang like elemental orisons
Through ages out of ages; words that fed
Love's hunger in the spirit; words that smote;
Thrilled words that echoed, and barbed words that clung;—
And every one of them was like a friend
Whose obstinate fidelity, well tried,
Had found at last and irresistibly
The way to her close conscience, and thereby
Revealed the unsubstantial Nemesis
That she had clutched and shuddered at so long;
And every one of them was like a real
And ringing voice, clear toned and absolute,
But of a love-subdued authority
That uttered thrice the plain significance
Of what had else been generously vague
And indolently true. It may have been
The triumph and the magic of the soul,
Unspeakably revealed, that finally
Had reconciled the grim probationing
Of wisdom with unalterable faith,

But she could feel—not knowing what it was,
For the sheer freedom of it—a new joy
That humanized the latent wizardry
Of his prophetic voice and put for it
The man within the music.

                                          So it came
To pass, like many a long-compelled emprise
That with its first accomplishment almost
Annihilates its own severity,
That she could find, whenever she might look,
The certified achievement of a love
That had endured, self-guarded and supreme,
To the glad end of all that wavering;
And she could see that now the flickering world
Of autumn was awake with sudden bloom,
New-born, perforce, of a slow bourgeoning.
And she had found what more than half had been
The grave-deluded, flesh-bewildered fear
Which men and women struggle to call faith,
To be the paid progression to an end
Whereat she knew the foresight and the strength
To glorify the gift of what was hers,
To vindicate the truth of what she was.
And had it come to her so suddenly?
There was a pity and a weariness
In asking that, and a great needlessness;
For now there were no wretched quivering strings
That held her to the churchyard any more:
There were no thoughts that flapped themselves like bats
Around her any more. The shield of love
Was clean, and she had paid enough to learn
How it had always been so. And the truth,
Like silence after some far victory,
Had come to her, and she had found it out
As if it were a vision, a thing born
So suddenly!—just as a flower is born,
Or as a world is born—so suddenly.

SAINTE-NITOUCHE

THOUGH not for common praise of him,
　　Nor yet for pride or charity,
Still would I make to Vanderberg
　　One tribute for his memory:

One honest warrant of a friend
　　Who found with him that flesh was grass—
Who neither blamed him in defect
　　Nor marveled how it came to pass;

Or why it ever was that he—
　　That Vanderberg, of all good men,
Should lose himself to find himself,
　　Straightway to lose himself again.

For we had buried Sainte-Nitouche,
　　And he had said to me that night:
"Yes, we have laid her in the earth,
　　But what of that?" And he was right.

And he had said: "We have a wife,
　　We have a child, we have a church;
'T would be a scurrilous way out
　　If we should leave them in the lurch.

"That's why I have you here with me
　　To-night: you know a talk may take
The place of bromide, cyanide,
　　Et cetera. For heaven's sake,

"Why do you look at me like that?
　　What have I done to freeze you so?
Dear man, you see where friendship means
　　A few things yet that you don't know;

"And you see partly why it is
    That I am glad for what is gone:
For Sainte-Nitouche and for the world
    In me that followed. What lives on—

"Well, here you have it: here at home—
    For even home will yet return.
You know the truth is on my side,
    And that will make the embers burn.

"I see them brighten while I speak,
    I see them flash,—and they are mine!
You do not know them, but I do:
    I know the way they used to shine.

"And I know more than I have told
    Of other life that is to be:
I shall have earned it when it comes,
    And when it comes I shall be free.

"Not as I was before she came,
    But farther on for having been
The servitor, the slave of her—
    The fool, you think. But there's your sin—

"Forgive me!—and your ignorance:
    Could you but have the vision here
That I have, you would understand
    As I do that all ways are clear

"For those who dare to follow them
    With earnest eyes and honest feet.
But Sainte-Nitouche has made the way
    For me, and I shall find it sweet.

"Sweet with a bitter sting left?—Yes,
    Bitter enough, God knows, at first;

But there are more steep ways than one
　To make the best look like the worst;

"And here is mine—the dark and hard,
　For me to follow, trust, and hold:
And worship, so that I may leave
　No broken story to be told.

"Therefore I welcome what may come,
　Glad for the days, the nights, the years."
An upward flash of ember-flame
　Revealed the gladness in his tears.

"You see them, but you know," said he,
　"Too much to be incredulous:
You know the day that makes us wise,
　The moment that makes fools of us.

"So I shall follow from now on
　The road that she has found for me:
The dark and starry way that leads
　Right upward, and eternally.

"Stumble at first? I may do that;
　And I may grope, and hate the night;
But there's a guidance for the man
　Who stumbles upward for the light,

"And I shall have it all from her,
　The foam-born child of innocence.
I feel you smiling while I speak,
　But that's of little consequence;

"For when we learn that we may find
　The truth where others miss the mark,
What is it worth for us to know
　That friends are smiling in the dark?

"Could we but share the lonely pride
    Of knowing, all would then be well;
But knowledge often writes itself
    In flaming words we cannot spell.

"And I, who have my work to do,
    Look forward; and I dare to see,
Far stretching and all mountainous,
    God's pathway through the gloom for me."

I found so little to say then
    That I said nothing.—"Say good-night,"
Said Vanderberg; "and when we meet
    To-morrow, tell me I was right.

"Forget the dozen other things
    That you have not the faith to say;
For now I know as well as you
    That you are glad to go away."

I could have blessed the man for that,
    And he could read me with a smile:
"You doubt," said he, "but if we live
    You'll know me in a little while."

He lived; and all as he foretold,
    I knew him—better than he thought:
My fancy did not wholly dig
    The pit where I believed him caught.

But yet he lived and laughed, and preached,
    And worked—as only players can:
He scoured the shrine that once was home
    And kept himself a clergyman.

The clockwork of his cold routine
    Put friends far off that once were near;

The five staccatos in his laugh
   Were too defensive and too clear;

The glacial sermons that he preached
   Were longer than they should have been;
And, like the man who fashioned them,
   The best were too divinely thin.

But still he lived, and moved, and had
   The sort of being that was his,
Till on a day the shrine of home
   For him was in the Mysteries:—

"My friend, there's one thing yet," said he,
   "And one that I have never shared
With any man that I have met;
   But you—you know me." And he stared

For a slow moment at me then
   With conscious eyes that had the gleam,
The shine, before the stroke:—"You know
   The ways of us, the way we dream:

"You know the glory we have won,
   You know the glamour we have lost;
You see me now, you look at me,—
   And yes, you pity me, almost;

"But never mind the pity—no,
   Confess the faith you can't conceal;
And if you frown, be not like one
   Of those who frown before they feel.

"For there is truth, and half truth,—yes,
   And there's a quarter truth, no doubt;
But mine was more than half. . . . You smile?
   You understand? You bear me out?

"You always knew that I was right—
    You are my friend—and I have tried
Your faith—your love."—The gleam grew small,
    The stroke was easy, and he died.

I saw the dim look change itself
    To one that never will be dim;
I saw the dead flesh to the grave,
    But that was not the last of him.

For what was his to live lives yet:
    Truth, quarter truth, death cannot reach;
Nor is it always what we know
    That we are fittest here to teach.

The fight goes on when fields are still,
    The triumph clings when arms are down;
The jewels of all coronets
    Are pebbles of the unseen crown;

The specious weight of loud reproof
    Sinks where a still conviction floats;
And on God's ocean after storm
    Time's wreckage is half pilot-boats;

And what wet faces wash to sight
    Thereafter feed the common moan;—
But Vanderberg no pilot had,
    Nor could have: he was all alone.

Unchallenged by the larger light
    The starry quest was his to make;
And of all ways that are for men,
    The starry way was his to take.

We grant him idle names enough
    To-day, but even while we frown

The fight goes on, the triumph clings,
  And there is yet the unseen crown

But was it his? Did Vanderberg
  Find half truth to be passion's thrall,
Or as we met him day by day,
  Was love triumphant, after all?

I do not know so much as that;
  I only know that he died right:
Saint Anthony nor Sainte-Nitouche
  Had ever smiled as he did—quite.

From

THE TOWN

DOWN

THE RIVER

1910

———◆◆———

To

Theodore

Roosevelt

THE MASTER *

(Lincoln)

A FLYING word from here and there
Had sown the name at which we sneered,
But soon the name was everywhere,
To be reviled and then revered:
A presence to be loved and feared,
We cannot hide it, or deny
That we, the gentlemen who jeered,
May be forgotten by and by.

He came when days were perilous
And hearts of men were sore beguiled;
And having made his note of us,
He pondered and was reconciled.
Was ever master yet so mild
As he, and so untamable?
We doubted, even when he smiled,
Not knowing what he knew so well.

He knew that undeceiving fate
Would shame us whom he served unsought;
He knew that he must wince and wait—
The jest of those for whom he fought;
He knew devoutly what he thought
Of us and of our ridicule;
He knew that we must all be taught
Like little children in a school.

We gave a glamour to the task
That he encountered and saw through,
But little of us did he ask,
And little did we ever do.

* Supposed to have been written not long after the
Civil War.

And what appears if we review
The season when we railed and chaffed?
It is the face of one who knew
That we were learning while we laughed.

The face that in our vision feels
Again the venom that we flung,
Transfigured to the world reveals
The vigilance to which we clung.
Shrewd, hallowed, harassed, and among
The mysteries that are untold,
The face we see was never young
Nor could it wholly have been old.

For he, to whom we had applied
Our shopman's test of age and worth,
Was elemental when he died,
As he was ancient at his birth:
The saddest among kings of earth,
Bowed with a galling crown, this man
Met rancor with a cryptic mirth,
Laconic—and Olympian.

The love, the grandeur, and the fame
Are bounded by the world alone;
The calm, the smouldering, and the flame
Of awful patience were his own:
With him they are forever flown
Past all our fond self-shadowings,
Wherewith we cumber the Unknown
As with inept, Icarian wings.

For we were not as other men:
'Twas ours to soar and his to see;
But we are coming down again,
And we shall come down pleasantly;
Nor shall we longer disagree
On what it is to be sublime,

But flourish in our perigee
And have one Titan at a time.

THE TOWN DOWN THE RIVER

I

SAID the Watcher by the Way
To the young and the unladen,
To the boy and to the maiden,
"God be with you both to-day.
First your song came ringing,
Now you come, you two,—
Knowing naught of what you do,
Or of what your dreams are bringing.

"O you children who go singing
To the Town down the River,
Where the millions cringe and shiver,
Tell me what you know to-day;
Tell me how far you are going,
Tell me how you find your way.
O you children who go dreaming,
Tell me what you dream to-day."

"He is old and we have heard him,"
Said the boy then to the maiden;
"He is old and heavy laden
With a load we throw away.
Care may come to find us,
Age may lay us low;
Still, we seek the light we know,
And the dead we leave behind us.

"Did he think that he would blind us
Into such a small believing

As to live without achieving,
When the lights have led so far?
Let him watch or let him wither,—
Shall he tell us where we are?
We know best who go together,
Downward, onward, and so far."

II

Said the Watcher by the Way
To the fiery folk that hastened,
To the loud and the unchastened,
"You are strong, I see, to-day.
Strength and hope may lead you
To the journey's end,—
Each to be the other's friend
If the Town should fail to need you.

"And are ravens there to feed you
In the Town down the River,
Where the gift appalls the giver
And youth hardens day by day?
O you brave and you unshaken,
Are you truly on your way?
And are sirens in the River,
That you come so far to-day?"

"You are old, and we have listened,"
Said the voice of one who halted;
"You are sage and self-exalted,
But your way is not our way.
You that cannot aid us
Give us words to eat.
Be assured that they are sweet,
And that we are as God made us.

"Not in vain have you delayed us,
Though the River still be calling

Through the twilight that is falling
And the Town be still so far.
By the whirlwind of your wisdom
Leagues are lifted as leaves are;
But a king without a kingdom
Fails us, who have come so far."

III

SAID the Watcher by the Way
To the slower folk who stumbled,
To the weak and the world-humbled,
"Tell me how you fare to-day.
Some with ardor shaken,
All with honor scarred,
Do you falter, finding hard
The far chance that you have taken?

"Or, do you at length awaken
To an antic retribution,
Goading to a new confusion
The drugged hopes of yesterday?
O you poor mad men that hobble,
Will you not return, or stay?
Do you trust, you broken people,
To a dawn without the day?"

"You speak well of what you know not,"
Muttered one; and then a second:
"You have begged and you have beckoned,
But you see us on our way.
Who are you to scold us,
Knowing what we know?
Jeremiah, long ago,
Said as much as you have told us.

"As we are, then, you behold us:
Derelicts of all conditions,

Poets, rogues, and sick physicians,
Plodding forward from afar;
Forward now into the darkness
Where the men before us are;
Forward, onward, out of grayness,
To the light that shone so far."

IV

SAID the Watcher by the Way
To some aged ones who lingered,
To the shrunken, the claw-fingered,
"So you come for me to-day."—
"Yes, to give you warning;
You are old," one said;
"You have old hairs on your head,
Fit for laurel, not for scorning.

"From the first of early morning
We have toiled along to find you;
We, as others, have maligned you,
But we need your scorn to-day.
By the light that we saw shining,
Let us not be lured alway;
Let us hear no River calling
When to-morrow is to-day."

"But your lanterns are unlighted
And the Town is far before you:
Let us hasten, I implore you,"
Said the Watcher by the Way.
"Long have I waited,
Longer have I known
That the Town would have its own,
And the call be for the fated.

"In the name of all created,
Let us hear no more, my brothers;

Are we older than all others?
Are the planets in our way?"—
"Hark," said one; "I hear the River,
Calling always, night and day."—
"Forward, then! The lights are shining,"
Said the Watcher by the Way.

CALVERLY'S

WE go no more to Calverly's,
For there the lights are few and low;
And who are there to see by them,
Or what they see, we do not know.
Poor strangers of another tongue
May now creep in from anywhere,
And we, forgotten, be no more
Than twilight on a ruin there.

We two, the remnant. All the rest
Are cold and quiet. You nor I,
Nor fiddle now, nor flagon-lid,
May ring them back from where they lie.
No fame delays oblivion
For them, but something yet survives:
A record written fair, could we
But read the book of scattered lives.

There'll be a page for Leffingwell,
And one for Lingard, the Moon-calf;
And who knows what for Clavering,
Who died because he couldn't laugh?
Who knows or cares? No sign is here,
No face, no voice, no memory;
No Lingard with his eerie joy,
No Clavering, no Calverly.

We cannot have them here with us
To say where their light lives are gone,
Or if they be of other stuff
Than are the moons of Ilion.
So, be their place of one estate
With ashes, echoes, and old wars,—
Or ever we be of the night,
Or we be lost among the stars.

LEFFINGWELL

I—The Lure

No, no—forget your Cricket and your Ant,
For I shall never set my name to theirs
That now bespeak the very sons and heirs
Incarnate of Queen Gossip and King Cant.
The case of Leffingwell is mixed, I grant,
And futile seems the burden that he bears;
But are we sounding his forlorn affairs
Who brand him parasite and sycophant?

I tell you, Leffingwell was more than these;
And if he prove a rather sorry knight,
What quiverings in the distance of what light
May not have lured him with high promises,
And then gone down?—He may have been deceived;
He may have lied,—he did; and he believed.

II—The Quickstep

THE dirge is over, the good work is done,
All as he would have had it, and we go;
And we who leave him say we do not know
How much is ended or how much begun.

So men have said before of many a one;
So men may say of us when Time shall throw
Such earth as may be needful to bestow
On you and me the covering hush we shun.

Well hated, better loved, he played and lost,
And left us; and we smile at his arrears;
And who are we to know what it all cost,
Or what we may have wrung from him, the buyer?
The pageant of his failure-laden years
Told ruin of high price. The place was higher.

III—REQUIESCAT

WE never knew the sorrow or the pain
Within him, for he seemed as one asleep—
Until he faced us with a dying leap,
And with a blast of paramount, profane,
And vehement valediction did explain
To each of us, in words that we shall keep,
Why we were not to wonder or to weep,
Or ever dare to wish him back again.

He may be now an amiable shade,
With merry fellow-phantoms unafraid
Around him—but we do not ask. We know
That he would rise and haunt us horribly,
And be with us o' nights of a certainty.
Did we not hear him when he told us so?

CLAVERING

I SAY no more for Clavering
    Than I should say of him who fails
To bring his wounded vessel home
    When reft of rudder and of sails;

I say no more than I should say
  Of any other one who sees
Too far for guidance of to-day,
  Too near for the eternities.

I think of him as I should think
  Of one who for scant wages played,
And faintly, a flawed instrument
  That fell while it was being made;

I think of him as one who fared,
  Unfaltering and undeceived,
Amid mirages of renown
  And urgings of the unachieved;

I think of him as one who gave
  To Lingard leave to be amused,
And listened with a patient grace
  That we, the wise ones, had refused;

I think of metres that he wrote
  For Cubit, the ophidian guest:
"What Lilith, or Dark Lady" . . . Well,
  Time swallows Cubit with the rest.

I think of last words that he said
  One midnight over Calverly:
"Good-by—good man." He was not good;
  So Clavering was wrong, you see.

I wonder what had come to pass
  Could he have borrowed for a spell
The fiery-frantic indolence
  That made a ghost of Leffingwell;

I wonder if he pitied us
  Who cautioned him till he was gray

To build his house with ours on earth
    And have an end of yesterday;

I wonder what it was we saw
    To make us think that we were strong;
I wonder if he saw too much,
    Or if he looked one way too long.

But when were thoughts or wonderings
    To ferret out the man within?
Why prate of what he seemed to be,
    And all that he might not have been?

He clung to phantoms and to friends,
    And never came to anything.
He left a wreath on Cubit's grave.
    I say no more for Clavering.

LINGARD AND THE STARS

The table hurled itself, to our surprise,
At Lingard, and anon rapped eagerly:
"When earth is cold and there is no more sea,
There will be what was Lingard. Otherwise,
Why lure the race to ruin through the skies?
And why have Leffingwell, or Calverly?"—
"I wish the ghost would give his name," said he;
And searching gratitude was in his eyes.

He stood then by the window for a time,
And only after the last midnight chime
Smote the day dead did he say anything:
"Come out, my little one, the stars are bright;
Come out, you lælaps, and inhale the night."
And so he went away with Clavering.

PASA THALASSA THALASSA

"The sea is everywhere the sea."

I

GONE—faded out of the story, the sea-faring friend I remember?
Gone for a decade, they say: never a word or a sign.
Gone with his hard red face that only his laughter could wrinkle,
Down where men go to be still, by the old way of the sea.

Never again will he come, with rings in his ears like a pirate,
Back to be living and seen, here with his roses and vines;
Here where the tenants are shadows and echoes of years uneventful,
Memory meets the event, told from afar by the sea.

Smoke that floated and rolled in the twilight away from the chimney
Floats and rolls no more. Wheeling and falling, instead,
Down with a twittering flash go the smooth and inscrutable swal-
lows,
Down to the place made theirs by the cold work of the sea.

Roses have had their day, and the dusk is on yarrow and worm-
wood—
Dusk that is over the grass, drenched with memorial dew;
Trellises lie like bones in a ruin that once was a garden,
Swallows have lingered and ceased, shadows and echoes are all.

II

WHERE is he lying to-night, as I turn away down to the valley,
Down where the lamps of men tell me the streets are alive?
Where shall I ask, and of whom, in the town or on land or on water,
News of a time and a place buried alike and with him?

Few now remain who may care, nor may they be wiser for caring,
Where or what manner the doom, whether by day or by night;
Whether in Indian deeps or on flood-laden fields of Atlantis,
Or by the roaring Horn, shrouded in silence he lies.

76

Few now remain who return by the weed-weary path to his cottage,
Drawn by the scene as it was—met by the chill and the change;
Few are alive who report, and few are alive who remember,
More of him now than a name carved somewhere on the sea.

"Where is he lying?" I ask, and the lights in the valley are nearer;
Down to the streets I go, down to the murmur of men.
Down to the roar of the sea in a ship may be well for another—
Down where he lies to-night, silent, and under the storms.

UNCLE ANANIAS

His words were magic and his heart was true,
    And everywhere he wandered he was blessed.
Out of all ancient men my childhood knew
    I choose him and I mark him for the best.
Of all authoritative liars, too,
    I crown him loveliest.

How fondly I remember the delight
    That always glorified him in the spring;
The joyous courage and the benedight
    Profusion of his faith in everything!
He was a good old man, and it was right
    That he should have his fling.

And often, underneath the apple-trees,
    When we surprised him in the summer time,
With what superb magnificence and ease
    He sinned enough to make the day sublime!
And if he liked us there about his knees,
    Truly it was no crime.

All summer long we loved him for the same
    Perennial inspiration of his lies;

77

And when the russet wealth of autumn came,
    There flew but fairer visions to our eyes—
Multiple, tropical, winged with a feathery flame,
    Like birds of paradise.

So to the sheltered end of many a year
    He charmed the seasons out with pageantry
Wearing upon his forehead, with no fear,
    The laurel of approved iniquity.
And every child who knew him, far or near,
    Did love him faithfully.

THE WHIP

THE doubt you fought so long
The cynic net you cast,
The tyranny, the wrong,
The ruin, they are past;
And here you are at last,
Your blood no longer vexed.
The coffin has you fast,
The clod will have you next.

But fear you not the clod,
Nor ever doubt the grave:
The roses and the sod
Will not forswear the wave.
The gift the river gave
Is now but theirs to cover:
The mistress and the slave
Are gone now, and the lover.

You left the two to find
Their own way to the brink
Then—shall I call you blind?—
You chose to plunge and sink.

God knows the gall we drink
Is not the mead we cry for,
Nor was it, I should think—
For you—a thing to die for.

Could we have done the same,
Had we been in your place?—
This funeral of your name
Throws no light on the case.
Could we have made the chase,
And felt then as you felt?—
But what's this on your face,
Blue, curious, like a welt?

There were some ropes of sand
Recorded long ago,
But none, I understand,
Of water. Is it so?
And she—she struck the blow,
You but a neck behind. . .
You saw the river flow—
Still, shall I call you blind?

THE WHITE LIGHTS

(BROADWAY, 1906)

WHEN in from Delos came the gold
That held the dream of Pericles,
When first Athenian ears were told
The tumult of Euripides,
When men met Aristophanes,
Who fledged them with immortal quills—
Here, where the time knew none of these,
There were some islands and some hills.

When Rome went ravening to see
The sons of mothers end their days,
When Flaccus bade Leuconoë
To banish her Chaldean ways,
When first the pearled, alembic phrase
Of Maro into music ran—
Here there was neither blame nor praise
For Rome, or for the Mantuan.

When Avon, like a faery floor,
Lay freighted, for the eyes of One,
With galleons laden long before
By moonlit wharves in Avalon—
Here, where the white lights have begun
To seethe a way for something fair,
No prophet knew, from what was done,
That there was triumph in the air.

EXIT

FOR what we owe to other days,
Before we poisoned him with praise,
May we who shrank to find him weak
Remember that he cannot speak.

For envy that we may recall,
And for our faith before the fall,
May we who are alive be slow
To tell what we shall never know.

For penance he would not confess,
And for the fateful emptiness
Of early triumph undermined,
May we now venture to be kind.

LEONORA

THEY have made for Leonora this low dwelling in the ground,
And with cedar they have woven the four walls round.
Like a little dryad hiding she'll be wrapped all in green,
Better kept and longer valued than by ways that would have been.

They will come with many roses in the early afternoon,
They will come with pinks and lilies and with Leonora soon;
And as long as beauty's garments over beauty's limbs are thrown,
There'll be lilies that are liars, and the rose will have its own.

There will be a wondrous quiet in the house that they have made,
And to-night will be a darkness in the place where she'll be laid;
But the builders, looking forward into time, could only see
Darker nights for Leonora than to-night shall ever be.

BUT FOR THE GRACE OF GOD

"There, but for the grace of God, goes . . ."

THERE is a question that I ask,
    And ask again:
What hunger was half-hidden by the mask
    That he wore then?

There was a word for me to say
    That I said not;
And in the past there was another day
    That I forgot:

A dreary, cold, unwholesome day,
    Racked overhead,—
As if the world were turning the wrong way
    And the sun dead:

A day that comes back well enough
    Now he is gone.
What then? Has memory no other stuff
    To seize upon?

Wherever he may wander now
    In his despair,
Would he be more contented in the slough
    If all were there?

And yet he brought a kind of light
    Into the room;
And when he left, a tinge of something bright
    Survived the gloom.

Why will he not be where he is,
    And not with me?
The hours that are my life are mine, not his,—
    Or used to be.

What numerous imps invisible
    Has he at hand,
Far-flying and forlorn as what they tell
    At his command?

What hold of weirdness or of worth
    Can he possess,
That he may speak from anywhere on earth
    His loneliness?

Shall I be caught and held again
    In the old net?—
He brought a sorry sunbeam with him then,
    But it beams yet.

THE SUNKEN CROWN

NOTHING will hold him longer—let him go;
Let him go down where others have gone down;
Little he cares whether we smile or frown,
Or if we know, or if we think we know.
The call is on him for his overthrow,
Say we; so let him rise, or let him drown.
Poor fool! He plunges for the sunken crown,
And we—we wait for what the plunge may show.

Well, we are safe enough. Why linger, then?
The watery chance was his, not ours. Poor fool!
Poor truant, poor Narcissus out of school;
Poor jest of Ascalon; poor king of men.—
The crown, if he be wearing it, may cool
His arrogance, and he may sleep again.

DOCTOR OF BILLIARDS

OF all among the fallen from on high,
We count you last and leave you to regain
Your born dominion of a life made vain
By three spheres of insidious ivory.
You dwindle to the lesser tragedy—
Content, you say. We call, but you remain.
Nothing alive gone wrong could be so plain,
Or quite so blasted with absurdity.

You click away the kingdom that is yours,
And you click off your crown for cap and bells;
You smile, who are still master of the feast,
And for your smile we credit you the least;
But when your false, unhallowed laugh occurs,
We seem to think there may be something else.

SHADRACH O'LEARY

O'LEARY was a poet—for a while:
He sang of many ladies frail and fair,
The rolling glory of their golden hair,
And emperors extinguished with a smile.
They foiled his years with many an ancient wile,
And if they limped, O'Leary didn't care:
He turned them loose and had them everywhere,
Undoing saints and senates with their guile.

But this was not the end. A year ago
I met him—and to meet was to admire:
Forgotten were the ladies and the lyre,
And the small, ink-fed Eros of his dream.
By questioning I found a man to know—
A failure spared, a Shadrach of the Gleam.

HOW ANNANDALE WENT OUT

"THEY called it Annandale—and I was there
To flourish, to find words, and to attend:
Liar, physician, hypocrite, and friend,
I watched him; and the sight was not so fair
As one or two that I have seen elsewhere:
An apparatus not for me to mend—
A wreck, with hell between him and the end,
Remained of Annandale; and I was there.

"I knew the ruin as I knew the man;
So put the two together, if you can,
Remembering the worst you know of me.
Now view yourself as I was, on the spot—
With a slight kind of engine. Do you see?
Like this . . . You wouldn't hang me? I thought not."

ALMA MATER

He knocked, and I beheld him at the door—
A vision for the gods to verify.
"What battered ancientry is this," thought I,
"And when, if ever, did we meet before?"
But ask him as I might, I got no more
For answer than a moaning and a cry:
Too late to parley, but in time to die,
He staggered, and lay shapeless on the floor.

When had I known him? And what brought him here?
Love, warning, malediction, hunger, fear?
Surely I never thwarted such as he?—
Again, what soiled obscurity was this:
Out of what scum, and up from what abyss,
Had they arrived—these rags of memory?

MINIVER CHEEVY

Miniver Cheevy, child of scorn,
   Grew lean while he assailed the seasons;
He wept that he was ever born,
   And he had reasons.

Miniver loved the days of old
   When swords were bright and steeds were prancing;
The vision of a warrior bold
   Would set him dancing.

Miniver sighed for what was not,
   And dreamed, and rested from his labors;
He dreamed of Thebes and Camelot,
   And Priam's neighbors.

Miniver mourned the ripe renown
  That made so many a name so fragrant;
He mourned Romance, now on the town,
  And Art, a vagrant.

Miniver loved the Medici,
  Albeit he had never seen one;
He would have sinned incessantly
  Could he have been one.

Miniver cursed the commonplace
  And eyed a khaki suit with loathing;
He missed the mediæval grace
  Of iron clothing.

Miniver scorned the gold he sought,
  But sore annoyed was he without it;
Miniver thought, and thought, and thought,
  And thought about it.

Miniver Cheevy, born too late,
  Scratched his head and kept on thinking;
Miniver coughed, and called it fate,
  And kept on drinking.

THE PILOT

From the Past and Unavailing
Out of cloudland we are steering:
After groping, after fearing,
Into starlight we come trailing,
And we find the stars are true.
Still, O comrade, what of you?
You are gone, but we are sailing,
And the old ways are all new.

For the Lost and Unreturning
We have drifted, we have waited;
Uncommanded and unrated,
We have tossed and wandered, yearning
For a charm that comes no more
From the old lights by the shore:
We have shamed ourselves in learning
What you knew so long before.

For the Breed of the Far-going
Who are strangers, and all brothers,
May forget no more than others
Who looked seaward with eyes flowing.
But are brothers to bewail
One who fought so foul a gale?
You have won beyond our knowing,
You are gone, but yet we sail.

VICKERY'S MOUNTAIN

BLUE in the west the mountain stands,
    And through the long twilight
Vickery sits with folded hands,
    And Vickery's eyes are bright.

Bright, for he knows what no man else
    On earth as yet may know:
There's a golden word that he never tells,
    And a gift that he will not show.

He dreams of honor and wealth and fame,
    He smiles, and well he may;
For to Vickery once a sick man came
    Who did not go away.

The day before the day to be,
　"Vickery," said the guest,
"You know as you live what's left of me—
　And you shall know the rest.

"You know as you live that I have come
　To this we call the end.
No doubt you have found me troublesome,
　But you've also found a friend;

"For we shall give and you shall take
　The gold that is in view;
The mountain there and I shall make
　A golden man of you.

"And you shall leave a friend behind
　Who neither frets nor feels;
And you shall move among your kind
　With hundreds at your heels.

"Now this that I have written here
　Tells all that need be told;
So, Vickery, take the way that's clear,
　And be a man of gold."

Vickery turned his eyes again
　To the far mountain-side,
And wept a tear for worthy men
　Defeated and defied.

Since then a crafty score of years
　Have come, and they have gone;
But Vickery counts no lost arrears:
　He lingers and lives on.

Blue in the west the mountain stands,
　Familiar as a face.
Blue, but Vickery knows what sands
　Are golden at its base.

He dreams and lives upon the day
　　When he shall walk with kings.
Vickery smiles—and well he may.
　　The life-caged linnet sings.

Vickery thinks the time will come
　　To go for what is his;
But hovering, unseen hands at home
　　Will hold him where he is.

There's a golden word that he never tells
　　And a gift that he will not show.
All to be given to some one else—
　　And Vickery not to know.

BON VOYAGE

Child of a line accurst
　　And old as Troy,
Bringer of best and worst
　　In wild alloy—
Light, like a linnet first,
　　He sang for joy.

Thrall to the gilded ease
　　Of every day,
Mocker of all degrees
　　And always gay,
Child of the Cyclades
　　And of Broadway—

Laughing and half divine
　　The boy began,
Drunk with a woodland wine
　　Thessalian:

But there was rue to twine
　　The pipes of Pan.

Therefore he skipped and flew
　　The more along,
Vivid and always new
　　And always wrong,
Knowing his only clew
　　A siren song.

Careless of each and all
　　He gave and spent:
Feast or a funeral
　　He laughed and went,
Laughing to be so small
　　In the event.

Told of his own deceit
　　By many a tongue,
Flayed for his long defeat
　　By being young,
Lured by the fateful sweet
　　Of songs unsung—

Knowing it in his heart,
　　But knowing not
The secret of an art
　　That few forgot,
He played the twinkling part
　　That was his lot.

And when the twinkle died,
　　As twinkles do,
He pushed himself aside
　　And out of view:
Out with the wind and tide,
　　Before we knew.

THE COMPANION

LET him answer as he will,
Or be lightsome as he may,
Now nor after shall he say
Worn-out words enough to kill,
Or to lull down by their craft,
Doubt, that was born yesterday,
When he lied and when she laughed.

Let him find another name
For the starlight on the snow,
Let him teach her till she know
That all seasons are the same,
And all sheltered ways are fair,—
Still, wherever she may go,
Doubt will have a dwelling there.

ATHERTON'S GAMBIT

THE master played the bishop's pawn,
For jest, while Atherton looked on;
The master played this way and that,
And Atherton, amazed thereat,
Said "Now I have a thing in view
That will enlighten one or two,
And make a difference or so
In what it is they do not know."

The morning stars together sang
And forth a mighty music rang—
Not heard by many, save as told
Again through magic manifold
By such a few as have to play
For others, in the Master's way,

The music that the Master made
When all the morning stars obeyed.

Atherton played the bishop's pawn
While more than one or two looked on;
Atherton played this way and that,
And many a friend, amused thereat,
Went on about his business
Nor cared for Atherton the less;
A few stood longer by the game,
With Atherton to them the same.

The morning stars are singing still,
To crown, to challenge, and to kill;
And if perforce there falls a voice
On pious ears that have no choice
Except to urge an erring hand
To wreak its homage on the land,
Who of us that is worth his while
Will, if he listen, more than smile?

Who of us, being what he is,
May scoff at others' ecstasies?
However we may shine to-day,
More-shining ones are on the way;
And so it were not wholly well
To be at odds with Azrael,—
Nor were it kind of any one
To sing the end of Atherton.

FOR A DEAD LADY

No more with overflowing light
Shall fill the eyes that now are faded,
Nor shall another's fringe with night
Their woman-hidden world as they did.

No more shall quiver down the days
The flowing wonder of her ways,
Whereof no language may requite
The shifting and the many-shaded.

The grace, divine, definitive,
Clings only as a faint forestalling;
The laugh that love could not forgive
Is hushed, and answers to no calling;
The forehead and the little ears
Have gone where Saturn keeps the years;
The breast where roses could not live
Has done with rising and with falling.

The beauty, shattered by the laws
That have creation in their keeping,
No longer trembles at applause,
Or over children that are sleeping;
And we who delve in beauty's lore
Know all that we have known before
Of what inexorable cause
Makes Time so vicious in his reaping.

TWO GARDENS IN LINNDALE

Two brothers, Oakes and Oliver,
Two gentle men as ever were,
Would roam no longer, but abide
In Linndale, where their fathers died,
And each would be a gardener.

"Now first we fence the garden through,
With this for me and that for you,"
Said Oliver.—"Divine!" said Oakes,
"And I, while I raise artichokes,
Will do what I was born to do."

"But this is not the soil, you know,"
Said Oliver, "to make them grow:
The parent of us, who is dead,
Compassionately shook his head
Once on a time and told me so."

"I hear you, gentle Oliver,"
Said Oakes, "and in your character
I find as fair a thing indeed
As ever bloomed and ran to seed
Since Adam was a gardener.

"Still, whatsoever I find there,
Forgive me if I do not share
The knowing gloom that you take on
Of one who doubted and is done:
For chemistry meets every prayer."

"Sometimes a rock will meet a plough,"
Said Oliver; "but anyhow
'Tis here we are, 'tis here we live,
With each to take and each to give:
There's no room for a quarrel now.

"I leave you in all gentleness
To science and a ripe success.
Now God be with you, brother Oakes,
With you and with your artichokes:
You have the vision, more or less."

"By fate, that gives to me no choice,
I have the vision and the voice:
Dear Oliver, believe in me,
And we shall see what we shall see;
Henceforward let us both rejoice."

"But first, while we have joy to spare
We'll plant a little here and there;

94

And if you be not in the wrong,
We'll sing together such a song
As no man yet sings anywhere."

They planted and with fruitful eyes
Attended each his enterprise.
"Now days will come and days will go,
And many a way be found, we know,"
Said Oakes, "and we shall sing, likewise."

"The days will go, the years will go,
And many a song be sung, we know,"
Said Oliver; "and if there be
Good harvesting for you and me,
Who cares if we sing loud or low?"

They planted once, and twice, and thrice,
Like amateurs in paradise;
And every spring, fond, foiled, elate,
Said Oakes, "We are in tune with Fate:
One season longer will suffice."

Year after year 'twas all the same:
With none to envy, none to blame,
They lived along in innocence,
Nor ever once forgot the fence,
Till on a day the Stranger came.

He came to greet them where they were,
And he too was a Gardener:
He stood between these gentle men,
He stayed a little while, and then
The land was all for Oliver.

'Tis Oliver who tills alone
Two gardens that are now his own;
'Tis Oliver who sows and reaps
And listens, while the other sleeps,
For songs undreamed of and unknown.

'Tis he, the gentle anchorite,
Who listens for them day and night;
But most he hears them in the dawn,
When from his trees across the lawn
Birds ring the chorus of the light.

He cannot sing without the voice,
But he may worship and rejoice
For patience in him to remain,
The chosen heir of age and pain,
Instead of Oakes—who had no choice.

'Tis Oliver who sits beside
The other's grave at eventide,
And smokes, and wonders what new race
Will have two gardens, by God's grace,
In Linndale, where their fathers died.

And often, while he sits and smokes,
He sees the ghost of gentle Oakes
Uprooting, with a restless hand,
Soft, shadowy flowers in a land
Of asphodels and artichokes.

THE REVEALER

(ROOSEVELT)

He turned aside to see the carcase of the
lion: and behold, there was a swarm of bees
and honey in the carcase of the lion. . . .
And the men of the city said unto him,
What is sweeter than honey? and what is
stronger than a lion?—*Judges,* 14.

THE palms of Mammon have disowned
The gift of our complacency;

The bells of ages have intoned
Again their rhythmic irony;
And from the shadow, suddenly,
'Mid echoes of decrepit rage,
The seer of our necessity
Confronts a Tyrian heritage.

Equipped with unobscured intent
He smiles with lions at the gate,
Acknowledging the compliment
Like one familiar with his fate;
The lions, having time to wait,
Perceive a small cloud in the skies,
Whereon they look, disconsolate,
With scared, reactionary eyes.

A shadow falls upon the land,—
They sniff, and they are like to roar;
For they will never understand
What they have never seen before.
They march in order to the door,
Not knowing the best thing to seek,
Nor caring if the gods restore
The lost composite of the Greek.

The shadow fades, the light arrives,
And ills that were concealed are seen;
The combs of long-defended hives
Now drip dishonored and unclean;
No Nazarite or Nazarene
Compels our questioning to prove
The difference that is between
Dead lions—or the sweet thereof.

But not for lions, live or dead,
Except as we are all as one,
Is he the world's accredited
Revealer of what we have done;

What You and I and Anderson
Are still to do is his reward;
If we go back when he is gone—
There is an Angel with a Sword.

He cannot close again the doors
That now are shattered for our sake;
He cannot answer for the floors
We crowd on, or for walls that shake;
He cannot wholly undertake
The cure of our immunity;
He cannot hold the stars, or make
Of seven years a century.

So Time will give us what we earn
Who flaunt the handful for the whole,
And leave us all that we may learn
Who read the surface for the soul;
And we'll be steering to the goal,
For we have said so to our sons:
When we who ride can pay the toll,
Time humors the far-seeing ones.

Down to our nose's very end
We see, and are invincible,—
Too vigilant to comprehend
The scope of what we cannot sell;
But while we seem to know as well
As we know dollars, or our skins,
The Titan may not always tell
Just where the boundary begins.

From

THE MAN

AGAINST

THE SKY

1916

———◆———

To

the Memory of

William Edward

Butler

FLAMMONDE

The man Flammonde, from God knows where,
With firm address and foreign air,
With news of nations in his talk
And something royal in his walk,
With glint of iron in his eyes,
But never doubt, nor yet surprise,
Appeared, and stayed, and held his head
As one by kings accredited.

Erect, with his alert repose
About him, and about his clothes,
He pictured all tradition hears
Of what we owe to fifty years.
His cleansing heritage of taste
Paraded neither want nor waste;
And what he needed for his fee
To live, he borrowed graciously.

He never told us what he was,
Or what mischance, or other cause,
Had banished him from better days
To play the Prince of Castaways.
Meanwhile he played surpassing well
A part, for most, unplayable;
In fine, one pauses, half afraid
To say for certain that he played.

For that, one may as well forego
Conviction as to yes or no;
Nor can I say just how intense
Would then have been the difference
To several, who, having striven
In vain to get what he was given,
Would see the stranger taken on
By friends not easy to be won.

Moreover, many a malcontent
He soothed and found munificent;
His courtesy beguiled and foiled
Suspicion that his years were soiled;
His mien distinguished any crowd,
His credit strengthened when he bowed;
And women, young and old, were fond
Of looking at the man Flammonde.

There was a woman in our town
On whom the fashion was to frown;
But while our talk renewed the tinge
Of a long-faded scarlet fringe,
The man Flammonde saw none of that,
And what he saw we wondered at—
That none of us, in her distress,
Could hide or find our littleness.

There was a boy that all agreed
Had shut within him the rare seed
Of learning. We could understand,
But none of us could lift a hand.
The man Flammonde appraised the youth,
And told a few of us the truth;
And thereby, for a little gold,
A flowered future was unrolled.

There were two citizens who fought
For years and years, and over nought;
They made life awkward for their friends,
And shortened their own dividends.
The man Flammonde said what was wrong
Should be made right; nor was it long
Before they were again in line,
And had each other in to dine.

And these I mention are but four
Of many out of many more.

So much for them. But what of him—
So firm in every look and limb?
What small satanic sort of kink
Was in his brain? What broken link
Withheld him from the destinies
That came so near to being his?

What was he, when we came to sift
His meaning, and to note the drift
Of incommunicable ways
That make us ponder while we praise?
Why was it that his charm revealed
Somehow the surface of a shield?
What was it that we never caught?
What was he, and what was he not?

How much it was of him we met
We cannot ever know; nor yet
Shall all he gave us quite atone
For what was his, and his alone;
Nor need we now, since he knew best,
Nourish an ethical unrest:
Rarely at once will nature give
The power to be Flammonde and live.

We cannot know how much we learn
From those who never will return,
Until a flash of unforeseen
Remembrance falls on what has been.
We've each a darkening hill to climb;
And this is why, from time to time
In Tilbury Town, we look beyond
Horizons for the man Flammonde.

THE GIFT OF GOD

BLESSED with a joy that only she
Of all alive shall ever know,
She wears a proud humility
For what it was that willed it so,—
That her degree should be so great
Among the favored of the Lord
That she may scarcely bear the weight
Of her bewildering reward.

As one apart, immune, alone,
Or featured for the shining ones,
And like to none that she has known
Of other women's other sons,—
The firm fruition of her need,
He shines anointed; and he blurs
Her vision, till it seems indeed
A sacrilege to call him hers.

She fears a little for so much
Of what is best, and hardly dares
To think of him as one to touch
With aches, indignities, and cares;
She sees him rather at the goal,
Still shining; and her dream foretells
The proper shining of a soul
Where nothing ordinary dwells.

Perchance a canvass of the town
Would find him far from flags and shouts,
And leave him only the renown
Of many smiles and many doubts;
Perchance the crude and common tongue
Would havoc strangely with his worth;
But she, with innocence unwrung,
Would read his name around the earth.

And others, knowing how this youth
Would shine, if love could make him great,
When caught and tortured for the truth
Would only writhe and hesitate;
While she, arranging for his days
What centuries could not fulfill,
Transmutes him with her faith and praise,
And has him shining where she will.

She crowns him with her gratefulness,
And says again that life is good;
And should the gift of God be less
In him than in her motherhood,
His fame, though vague, will not be small,
As upward through her dream he fares,
Half clouded with a crimson fall
Of roses thrown on marble stairs.

THE CLINGING VINE

"BE calm? And was I frantic?
    You'll have me laughing soon.
I'm calm as this Atlantic,
    And quiet as the moon;
I may have spoken faster
    Than once, in other days;
For I've no more a master,
    And now—'Be calm,' he says.

"Fear not, fear no commotion,—
    I'll be as rocks and sand;
The moon and stars and ocean
    Will envy my command;
No creature could be stiller
    In any kind of place

Than I . . . No, I'll not kill her;
  Her death is in her face.

"Be happy while she has it,
  For she'll not have it long;
A year, and then you'll pass it,
  Preparing a new song.
And I'm a fool for prating
  Of what a year may bring,
When more like her are waiting
  For more like you to sing.

"You mock me with denial,
  You mean to call me hard?
You see no room for trial
  When all my doors are barred?
You say, and you'd say dying,
  That I dream what I know;
And sighing, and denying,
  You'd hold my hand and go.

"You scowl—and I don't wonder;
  I spoke too fast again;
But you'll forgive one blunder,
  For you are like most men:
You are,—or so you've told me,
  So many mortal times,
That heaven ought not to hold me
  Accountable for crimes.

"Be calm? Was I unpleasant?
  Then I'll be more discreet,
And grant you, for the present,
  The balm of my defeat:
What she, with all her striving,
  Could not have brought about,
You've done. Your own contriving
  Has put the last light out.

"If she were the whole story,
  If worse were not behind,
I'd creep with you to glory,
  Believing I was blind;
I'd creep, and go on seeming
  To be what I despise.
You laugh, and say I'm dreaming,
  And all your laughs are lies.

"Are women mad? A few are,
  And if it's true you say—
If most men are as you are—
  We'll all be mad some day.
Be calm—and let me finish;
  There's more for you to know.
I'll talk while you diminish,
  And listen while you grow.

"There was a man who married
  Because he couldn't see;
And all his days he carried
  The mark of his degree.
But you—you came clear-sighted,
  And found truth in my eyes;
And all my wrongs you've righted
  With lies, and lies, and lies.

"You've killed the last assurance
  That once would have me strive
To rouse an old endurance
  That is no more alive.
It makes two people chilly
  To say what we have said,
But you—you'll not be silly
  And wrangle for the dead.

"You don't? You never wrangle?
  Why scold then,—or complain?·

More words will only mangle
　　What you've already slain.
Your pride you can't surrender?
　　My name—for that you fear?
Since when were men so tender,
　　And honor so severe?

"No more—Ill never bear it.
　　I'm going. I'm like ice.
My burden? You would share it?
　　Forbid the sacrifice!
Forget so quaint a notion,
　　And let no more be told;
For moon and stars and ocean
　　And you and I are cold."

CASSANDRA

I HEARD one who said: "Verily,
　　What word have I for children here?
Your Dollar is your only Word,
　　The wrath of it your only fear.

"You build it altars tall enough
　　To make you see, but you are blind;
You cannot leave it long enough
　　To look before you or behind.

"When Reason beckons you to pause,
　　You laugh and say that you know best;
But what it is you know, you keep
　　As dark as ingots in a chest.

"You laugh and answer, 'We are young;
　　O leave us now, and let us grow.'—

Not asking how much more of this
    Will Time endure or Fate bestow.

"Because a few complacent years
    Have made your peril of your pride,
Think you that you are to go on
    Forever pampered and untried?

"What lost eclipse of history,
    What bivouac of the marching stars,
Has given the sign for you to see
    Millenniums and last great wars?

"What unrecorded overthrow
    Of all the world has ever known,
Or ever been, has made itself
    So plain to you, and you alone?

"Your Dollar, Dove and Eagle made
    A Trinity that even you
Rate higher than you rate yourselves;
    It pays, it flatters, and it's new.

"And though your very flesh and blood
    Be what your Eagle eats and drinks,
You'll praise him for the best of birds,
    Not knowing what the Eagle thinks.

"The power is yours, but not the sight;
    You see not upon what you tread;
You have the ages for your guide,
    But not the wisdom to be led.

"Think you to tread forever down
    The merciless old verities?
And are you never to have eyes
    To see the world for what it is?

"Are you to pay for what you have
    With all you are?"—No other word
We caught, but with a laughing crowd
    Moved on. None heeded, and few heard.

JOHN GORHAM

"TELL me what you're doing over here, John Gorham,
Sighing hard and seeming to be sorry when you're not;
Make me laugh or let me go now, for long faces in the moonlight
Are a sign for me to say again a word that you forgot."—

"I'm over here to tell you what the moon already
May have said or maybe shouted ever since a year ago;
I'm over here to tell you what you are, Jane Wayland,
And to make you rather sorry, I should say, for being so."—

"Tell me what you're saying to me now, John Gorham,
Or you'll never see as much of me as ribbons any more;
I'll vanish in as many ways as I have toes and fingers,
And you'll not follow far for one where flocks have been before."—

"I'm sorry now you never saw the flocks, Jane Wayland,
But you're the one to make of them as many as you need.
And then about the vanishing. It's I who mean to vanish;
And when I'm here no longer you'll be done with me indeed."—

"That's a way to tell me what I am, John Gorham!
How am I to know myself until I make you smile?
Try to look as if the moon were making faces at you,
And a little more as if you meant to stay a little while."—

"You are what it is that over rose-blown gardens
Makes a pretty flutter for a season in the sun;

You are what it is that with a mouse, Jane Wayland,
Catches him and lets him go and eats him up for fun."—

"Sure I never took you for a mouse, John Gorham;
All you say is easy, but so far from being true
That I wish you wouldn't ever be again the one to think so;
For it isn't cats and butterflies that I would be to you."—

"All your little animals are in one picture—
One I've had before me since a year ago to-night;
And the picture where they live will be of you, Jane Wayland,
Till you find a way to kill them or to keep them out of sight."—

"Won't you ever see me as I am, John Gorham,
Leaving out the foolishness and all I never meant?
Somewhere in me there's a woman, if you know the way to find her.
Will you like me any better if I prove it and repent?"—

"I doubt if I shall ever have the time, Jane Wayland;
And I dare say all this moonlight lying round us might as well
Fall for nothing on the shards of broken urns that are forgotten,
As on two that have no longer much of anything to tell."

HILLCREST

(To Mrs. Edward MacDowell)

No sound of any storm that shakes
Old island walls with older seas
Comes here where now September makes
An island in a sea of trees.

Between the sunlight and the shade
A man may learn till he forgets
The roaring of a world remade,
And all his ruins and regrets;

And if he still remembers here
Poor fights he may have won or lost,—
If he be ridden with the fear
Of what some other fight may cost,—

If, eager to confuse too soon,
What he has known with what may be,
He reads a planet out of tune
For cause of his jarred harmony,—

If here he venture to unroll
His index of adagios,
And he be given to console
Humanity with what he knows,—

He may by contemplation learn
A little more than what he knew,
And even see great oaks return
To acorns out of which they grew.

He may, if he but listen well,
Through twilight and the silence here,
Be told what there are none may tell
To vanity's impatient ear;

And he may never dare again
Say what awaits him, or be sure
What sunlit labyrinth of pain
He may not enter and endure.

Who knows to-day from yesterday
May learn to count no thing too strange:
Love builds of what Time takes away,
Till Death itself is less than Change.

Who sees enough in his duress
May go as far as dreams have gone;

Who sees a little may do less
Than many who are blind have done;

Who sees unchastened here the soul
Triumphant has no other sight
Than has a child who sees the whole
World radiant with his own delight.

Far journeys and hard wandering
Await him in whose crude surmise
Peace, like a mask, hides everything
That is and has been from his eyes;

And all his wisdom is unfound,
Or like a web that error weaves
On airy looms that have a sound
No louder now than falling leaves.

OLD KING COLE

In Tilbury Town did Old King Cole
A wise old age anticipate,
Desiring, with his pipe and bowl,
No Khan's extravagant estate.
No crown annoyed his honest head,
No fiddlers three were called or needed,
For two disastrous heirs instead
Made music more than ever three did.

Bereft of her with whom his life
Was harmony without a flaw,
He took no other for a wife,
Nor sighed for any that he saw;
And if he doubted his two sons,
And heirs, Alexis and Evander,

He might have been as doubtful once
Of Robert Burns and Alexander.

Alexis, in his early youth,
Began to steal—from old and young.
Likewise Evander, and the truth
Was like a bad taste on his tongue.
Born thieves and liars, their affair
Seemed only to be tarred with evil—
The most insufferable pair
Of scamps that ever cheered the devil.

The world went on, their fame went on,
And they went on—from bad to worse;
Till, goaded hot with nothing done,
And each accoutred with a curse,
The friends of Old King Cole, by twos,
And fours, and sevens, and elevens,
Pronounced unalterable views
Of doings that were not of heaven's.

And having learned again whereby
Their baleful zeal had come about,
King Cole met many a wrathful eye
So kindly that its wrath went out—
Or partly out. Say what they would,
He seemed the more to court their candor;
But never told what kind of good
Was in Alexis and Evander.

And Old King Cole, with many a puff
That haloed his urbanity,
Would smoke till he had smoked enough,
And listen most attentively.
He beamed as with an inward light
That had the Lord's assurance in it;
And once a man was there all night,
Expecting something every minute.

But whether from too little thought,
Or too much fealty to the bowl,
A dim reward was all he got
For sitting up with Old King Cole.
"Though mine," the father mused aloud,
"Are not the sons I would have chosen,
Shall I, less evilly endowed,
By their infirmity be frozen?

"They'll have a bad end, I'll agree,
But I was never born to groan;
For I can see what I can see,
And I'm accordingly alone.
With open heart and open door,
I love my friends, I like my neighbors;
But if I try to tell you more,
Your doubts will overmatch my labors.

"This pipe would never make me calm,
This bowl my grief would never drown.
For grief like mine there is no balm
In Gilead, or in Tilbury Town.
And if I see what I can see,
I know not any way to blind it;
Nor more if any way may be
For you to grope or fly to find it.

"There may be room for ruin yet,
And ashes for a wasted love;
Or, like One whom you may forget,
I may have meat you know not of.
And if I'd rather live than weep
Meanwhile, do you find that surprising?
Why, bless my soul, the man's asleep!
That's good. The sun will soon be rising."

BEN JONSON ENTERTAINS
A MAN FROM STRATFORD

You are a friend then, as I make it out,
Of our man Shakespeare, who alone of us
Will put an ass's head in Fairyland
As he would add a shilling to more shillings,
All most harmonious,—and out of his
Miraculous inviolable increase
Fills Ilion, Rome, or any town you like
Of olden time with timeless Englishmen;
And I must wonder what you think of him—
All you down there where your small Avon flows
By Stratford, and where you're an Alderman.
Some, for a guess, would have him riding back
To be a farrier there, or say a dyer;
Or maybe one of your adept surveyors;
Or like enough the wizard of all tanners.
Not you—no fear of that; for I discern
In you a kindling of the flame that saves—
The nimble element, the true caloric;
I see it, and was told of it, moreover,
By our discriminate friend himself, no other.
Had you been one of the sad average,
As he would have it,—meaning, as I take it,
The sinew and the solvent of our Island,
You'd not be buying beer for this Terpander's
Approved and estimated friend Ben Jonson;
He'd never foist it as a part of his
Contingent entertainment of a townsman
While he goes off rehearsing, as he must,
If he shall ever be the Duke of Stratford.
And my words are no shadow on your town—
Far from it; for one town's as like another
As all are unlike London. Oh, he knows it,—
And there's the Stratford in him; he denies it,
And there's the Shakespeare in him. So, God help him!
I tell him he needs Greek; but neither God

Nor Greek will help him. Nothing will help that man.
You see the fates have given him so much,
He must have all or perish,—or look out
Of London, where he sees too many lords.
They're part of half what ails him: I suppose
There's nothing fouler down among the demons
Than what it is he feels when he remembers
The dust and sweat and ointment of his calling
With his lords looking on and laughing at him.
King as he is, he can't be king *de facto,*
And that's as well, because he wouldn't like it;
He'd frame a lower rating of men then
Than he has now; and after that would come
An abdication or an apoplexy.
He can't be king, not even king of Stratford,—
Though half the world, if not the whole of it,
May crown him with a crown that fits no king
Save Lord Apollo's homesick emissary:
Not there on Avon, or on any stream
Where Naiads and their white arms are no more,
Shall he find home again. It's all too bad.
But there's a comfort, for he'll have that House—
The best you ever saw; and he'll be there
Anon, as you're an Alderman. Good God!
He makes me lie awake o'nights and laugh.

And you have known him from his origin,
You tell me; and a most uncommon urchin
He must have been to the few seeing ones—
A trifle terrifying, I dare say,
Discovering a world with his man's eyes,
Quite as another lad might see some finches,
If he looked hard and had an eye for nature.
But this one had his eyes and their foretelling,
And he had you to fare with, and what else?
He must have had a father and a mother—
In fact I've heard him say so—and a dog,
As a boy should, I venture; and the dog,

Most likely, was the only man who knew him.
A dog, for all I know, is what he needs
As much as anything right here to-day,
To counsel him about his disillusions,
Old aches, and parturitions of what's coming,—
A dog of orders, an emeritus,
To wag his tail at him when he comes home,
And then to put his paws up on his knees
And say, "For God's sake, what's it all about?"

I don't know whether he needs a dog or not—
Or what he needs. I tell him he needs Greek;
I'll talk of rules and Aristotle with him,
And if his tongue's at home he'll say to that,
"I have your word that Aristotle knows,
And you mine that I don't know Aristotle."
He's all at odds with all the unities,
And what's yet worse, it doesn't seem to matter;
He treads along through Time's old wilderness
As if the tramp of all the centuries
Had left no roads—and there are none, for him;
He doesn't see them, even with those eyes,—
And that's a pity, or I say it is.
Accordingly we have him as we have him—
Going his way, the way that he goes best,
A pleasant animal with no great noise
Or nonsense anywhere to set him off—
Save only divers and inclement devils
Have made of late his heart their dwelling place.
A flame half ready to fly out sometimes
At some annoyance may be fanned up in him,
But soon it falls, and when it falls goes out;
He knows how little room there is in there
For crude and futile animosities,
And how much for the joy of being whole,
And how much for long sorrow and old pain.
On our side there are some who may be given
To grow old wondering what he thinks of us

And some above us, who are, in his eyes,
Above himself,—and that's quite right and English.
Yet here we smile, or disappoint the gods
Who made it so: the gods have always eyes
To see men scratch; and they see one down here
Who itches, manor-bitten to the bone,
Albeit he knows himself—yes, yes, he knows—
The lord of more than England and of more
Than all the seas of England in all time
Shall ever wash. D'ye wonder that I laugh?
He sees me, and he doesn't seem to care;
And why the devil should he? I can't tell you.

I'll meet him out alone of a bright Sunday,
Trim, rather spruce, and quite the gentleman.
"What ho, my lord!" say I. He doesn't hear me;
Wherefore I have to pause and look at him.
He's not enormous, but one looks at him.
A little on the round if you insist,
For now, God save the mark, he's growing old;
He's five and forty, and to hear him talk
These days you'd call him eighty; then you'd add
More years to that. He's old enough to be
The father of a world, and so he is.
"Ben, you're a scholar, what's the time of day?"
Says he; and there shines out of him again
An aged light that has no age or station—
The mystery that's his—a mischievous
Half-mad serenity that laughs at fame
For being won so easy, and at friends
Who laugh at him for what he wants the most,
And for his dukedom down in Warwickshire;—
By which you see we're all a little jealous. . . .
Poor Greene! I fear the color of his name
Was even as that of his ascending soul;
And he was one where there are many others,—
Some scrivening to the end against their fate,
Their puppets all in ink and all to die there;

And some with hands that once would shade an eye
That scanned Euripides and Æschylus
Will reach by this time for a pot-house mop
To slush their first and last of royalties.
Poor devils! and they all play to his hand;
For so it was in Athens and old Rome.
But that's not here or there; I've wandered off.
Greene does it, or I'm careful. Where's that boy?

Yes, he'll go back to Stratford. And we'll miss him?
Dear sir, there'll be no London here without him.
We'll all be riding, one of these fine days,
Down there to see him—and his wife won't like us;
And then we'll think of what he never said
Of women—which, if taken all in all
With what he did say, would buy many horses.
Though nowadays he's not so much for women:
"So few of them," he says, "are worth the guessing."
But there's a worm at work when he says that,
And while he says it one feels in the air
A deal of circumambient hocus-pocus.
They've had him dancing till his toes were tender,
And he can feel 'em now, come chilly rains.
There's no long cry for going into it,
However, and we don't know much about it.
But you in Stratford, like most here in London,
Have more now in the *Sonnets* than you paid for;
He's put one there with all her poison on,
To make a singing fiction of a shadow
That's in his life a fact, and always will be.
But she's no care of ours, though Time, I fear,
Will have a more reverberant ado
About her than about another one
Who seems to have decoyed him, married him,
And sent him scuttling on his way to London,—
With much already learned, and more to learn,
And more to follow. Lord! how I see him now,
Pretending, maybe trying, to be like us.

Whatever he may have meant, we never had him;
He failed us, or escaped, or what you will,—
And there was that about him (God knows what,—
We'd flayed another had he tried it on us)
That made as many of us as had wits
More fond of all his easy distances
Than one another's noise and clap-your-shoulder.
But think you not, my friend, he'd never talk!
Talk? He was eldritch at it; and we listened—
Thereby acquiring much we knew before
About ourselves, and hitherto had held
Irrelevant, or not prime to the purpose.

And there were some, of course, and there be now,
Disordered and reduced amazedly
To resignation by the mystic seal
Of young finality the gods had laid
On everything that made him a young demon;
And one or two shot looks at him already
As he had been their executioner;
And once or twice he was, not knowing it,—
Or knowing, being sorry for poor clay
And saying nothing. . . . Yet, for all his engines,
You'll meet a thousand of an afternoon
Who strut and sun themselves and see around 'em
A world made out of more that has a reason
Than his, I swear, that he sees here to-day;
Though he may scarcely give a Fool an exit
But we mark how he sees in everything
A law that, given we flout it once too often,
Brings fire and iron down on our naked heads.
To me it looks as if the power that made him,
For fear of giving all things to one creature,
Left out the first,—faith, innocence, illusion,
Whatever 'tis that keeps us out o' Bedlam,—
And thereby, for his too consuming vision,
Empowered him out of nature; though to see him,
You'd never guess what's going on inside him.

He'll break out some day like a keg of ale
With too much independent frenzy in it;
And all for cellaring what he knows won't keep,
And what he'd best forget—but that he can't.
You'll have it, and have more than I'm foretelling;
And there'll be such a roaring at the Globe
As never stunned the bleeding gladiators.
He'll have to change the color of its hair
A bit, for now he calls it Cleopatra.
Black hair would never do for Cleopatra.
But you and I are not yet two old women,
And you're a man of office. What he does
Is more to you than how it is he does it,—
And that's what the Lord God has never told him.
They work together, and the Devil helps 'em;
They do it of a morning, or if not,
They do it of a night; in which event
He's peevish of a morning. He seems old;
He's not the proper stomach or the sleep—
And they're two sovran agents to conserve him
Against the fiery art that has no mercy
But what's in that prodigious grand new House.
I gather something happening in his boyhood
Fulfilled him with a boy's determination
To make all Stratford 'ware of him. Well, well,
I hope at last he'll have his joy of it,
And all his pigs and sheep and bellowing beeves,
And frogs and owls and unicorns, moreover,
Be less than hell to his attendant ears.
Oh, past a doubt we'll all go down to see him.

He may be wise. With London two days off,
Down there some wind of heaven may yet revive him:
But there's no quickening breath from anywhere
Shall make of him again the poised young faun
From Warwickshire, who'd made, it seems, already
A legend of himself before I came

To blink before the last of his first lightning.
Whatever there be, there'll be no more of that;
The coming on of his old monster Time
Has made him a still man; and he has dreams
Were fair to think on once, and all found hollow.
He knows how much of what men paint themselves
Would blister in the light of what they are;
He sees how much of what was great now shares
An eminence transformed and ordinary;
He knows too much of what the world has hushed
In others, to be loud now for himself;
He knows now at what height low enemies
May reach his heart, and high friends let him fall;
But what not even such as he may know
Bedevils him the worst: his lark may sing
At heaven's gate how he will, and for as long
As joy may listen, but *he* sees no gate,
Save one whereat the spent clay waits a little
Before the churchyard has it, and the worm.
Not long ago, late in an afternoon,
I came on him unseen down Lambeth way,
And on my life I was afear'd of him:
He gloomed and mumbled like a soul from Tophet,
His hands behind him and his head bent solemn.
"What is it now," said I,—"another woman?"
That made him sorry for me, and he smiled.
"No, Ben," he mused; "it's Nothing. It's all Nothing.
We come, we go; and when we're done, we're done.
Spiders and flies—we're mostly one or t'other—
We come, we go; and when we're done, we're done."
"By God, you sing that song as if you knew it!"
Said I, by way of cheering him; "what ails ye?"
"I think I must have come down here to think,"
Says he to that, and pulls his little beard;
"Your fly will serve as well as anybody,
And what's his hour? He flies, and flies, and flies,
And in his fly's mind has a brave appearance;

And then your spider gets him in her net,
And eats him out, and hangs him up to dry.
That's Nature, the kind mother of us all.
And then your slattern housemaid swings her broom,
And where's your spider? And that's Nature, also.
It's Nature, and it's Nothing. It's all Nothing.
It's all a world where bugs and emperors
Go singularly back to the same dust,
Each in his time; and the old, ordered stars
That sang together, Ben, will sing the same
Old stave to-morrow."

      When he talks like that,
There's nothing for a human man to do
But lead him to some grateful nook like this
Where we be now, and there to make him drink.
He'll drink, for love of me, and then be sick;
A sad sign always in a man of parts,
And always very ominous. The great
Should be as large in liquor as in love,—
And our great friend is not so large in either:
One disaffects him, and the other fails him;
Whatso he drinks that has an antic in it,
He's wondering what's to pay in his insides;
And while his eyes are on the Cyprian
He's fribbling all the time with that damned House.
We laugh here at his thrift, but after all
It may be thrift that saves him from the devil;
God gave it, anyhow,—and we'll suppose
He knew the compound of his handiwork.
To-day the clouds are with him, but anon
He'll out of 'em enough to shake the tree
Of life itself and bring down fruit unheard-of,—
And, throwing in the bruised and whole together,
Prepare a wine to make us drunk with wonder:
And if he live, there'll be a sunset spell
Thrown over him as over a glassed lake
That yesterday was all a black wild water.

God send he live to give us, if no more,
What now's a-rampage in him, and exhibit,
With a decent half-allegiance to the ages
An earnest of at least a casual eye
Turned once on what he owes to Gutenberg,
And to the fealty of more centuries
Than are as yet a picture in our vision.
"There's time enough,—I'll do it when I'm old,
And we're immortal men," he says to that;
And then he says to me, "Ben, what's 'immortal'?
Think you by any force of ordination
It may be nothing of a sort more noisy
Than a small oblivion of component ashes
That of a dream-addicted world was once
A moving atomy much like your friend here?"
Nothing will help that man. To make him laugh,
I said then he was a mad mountebank,—
And by the Lord I nearer made him cry.
I could have eat an eft then, on my knees,
Tail, claws, and all of him; for I had stung
The king of men, who had no sting for me,
And I had hurt him in his memories;
And I say now, as I shall say again,
I love the man this side idolatry.

He'll do it when he's old, he says. I wonder.
He may not be so ancient as all that.
For such as he, the thing that is to do
Will do itself,—but there's a reckoning;
The sessions that are now too much his own,
The roiling inward of a stilled outside,
The churning out of all those blood-fed lines,
The nights of many schemes and little sleep,
The full brain hammered hot with too much thinking,
The vexed heart over-worn with too much aching,—
This weary jangling of conjoined affairs
Made out of elements that have no end.
And all confused at once, I understand,

Is not what makes a man to live forever.
O no, not now! He'll not be going now:
There'll be time yet for God knows what explosions
Before he goes. He'll stay awhile. Just wait:
Just wait a year or two for Cleopatra,
For she's to be a balsam and a comfort;
And that's not all a jape of mine now, either.
For granted once the old way of Apollo
Sings in a man, he may then, if he's able,
Strike unafraid whatever strings he will
Upon the last and wildest of new lyres;
Nor out of his new magic, though it hymn
The shrieks of dungeoned hell, shall he create
A madness or a gloom to shut quite out
A cleaving daylight, and a last great calm
Triumphant over shipwreck and all storms.
He might have given Aristotle creeps,
But surely would have given him his *katharsis*.

He'll not be going yet. There's too much yet
Unsung within the man. But when he goes,
I'd stake ye coin o' the realm his only care
For a phantom world he sounded and found wanting
Will be a portion here, a portion there,
Of this or that thing or some other thing
That has a patent and intrinsical
Equivalence in those egregious shillings.
And yet he knows, God help him! Tell me, now,
If ever there was anything let loose
On earth by gods or devils heretofore
Like this mad, careful, proud, indifferent Shakespeare!
Where was it, if it ever was? By heaven,
'Twas never yet in Rhodes or Pergamon—
In Thebes or Nineveh, a thing like this!
No thing like this was ever out of England;
And that he knows. I wonder if he cares.
Perhaps he does. . . . O Lord, that House in Stratford!

EROS TURANNOS

She fears him, and will always ask
    What fated her to choose him;
She meets in his engaging mask
    All reasons to refuse him;
But what she meets and what she fears
Are less than are the downward years,
Drawn slowly to the foamless weirs
    Of age, were she to lose him.

Between a blurred sagacity
    That once had power to sound him,
And Love, that will not let him be
    The Judas that she found him,
Her pride assuages her almost,
As if it were alone the cost.—
He sees that he will not be lost,
    And waits and looks around him.

A sense of ocean and old trees
    Envelops and allures him;
Tradition, touching all he sees,
    Beguiles and reassures him;
And all her doubts of what he says
Are dimmed with what she knows of days—
Till even prejudice delays
    And fades, and she secures him.

The falling leaf inaugurates
    The reign of her confusion;
The pounding wave reverberates
    The dirge of her illusion;
And home, where passion lived and died,
Becomes a place where she can hide,
While all the town and harbor side
    Vibrate with her seclusion.

We tell you, tapping on our brows,
    The story as it should be,—
As if the story of a house
    Were told, or ever could be;
We'll have no kindly veil between
Her visions and those we have seen,—
As if we guessed what hers have been,
    Or what they are or would be.

Meanwhile we do no harm; for they
    That with a god have striven,
Not hearing much of what we say,
    Take what the god has given;
Though like waves breaking it may be,
Or like a changed familiar tree,
Or like a stairway to the sea
    Where down the blind are driven.

OLD TRAILS

(Washington Square)

I MET him, as one meets a ghost or two,
Between the gray Arch and the old Hotel.
"King Solomon was right, there's nothing new,"
Said he. "Behold a ruin who meant well."

He led me down familiar steps again,
Appealingly, and set me in a chair.
"My dreams have all come true to other men,"
Said he; "God lives, however, and why care?

"An hour among the ghosts will do no harm."
He laughed, and something glad within me sank.
I may have eyed him with a faint alarm,
For now his laugh was lost in what he drank.

"They chill things here with ice from hell," he said;
"I might have known it." And he made a face
That showed again how much of him was dead,
And how much was alive and out of place,

And out of reach. He knew as well as I
That all the words of wise men who are skilled
In using them are not much to defy
What comes when memory meets the unfulfilled.

What evil and infirm perversity
Had been at work with him to bring him back?
Never among the ghosts, assuredly,
Would he originate a new attack;

Never among the ghosts, or anywhere,
Till what was dead of him was put away,
Would he attain to his offended share
Of honor among others of his day.

"You ponder like an owl," he said at last;
"You always did, and here you have a cause.
For I'm a confirmation of the past,
A vengeance, and a flowering of what was.

"Sorry? Of course you are, though you compress,
With even your most impenetrable fears,
A placid and a proper consciousness
Of anxious angels over my arrears.

"I see them there against me in a book
As large as hope, in ink that shines by night
Surely I see; but now I'd rather look
At you, and you are not a pleasant sight.

"Forbear, forgive. Ten years are on my soul,
And on my conscience. I've an incubus:

My one distinction, and a parlous toll
To glory; but hope lives on clamorous.

" 'Twas hope, though heaven I grant you knows of what—
The kind that blinks and rises when it falls,
Whether it sees a reason why or not—
That heard Broadway's hard-throated siren-calls;

" 'Twas hope that brought me through December storms,
To shores again where I'll not have to be
A lonely man with only foreign worms
To cheer him in his last obscurity.

"But what it was that hurried me down here
To be among the ghosts, I leave to you.
My thanks are yours, no less, for one thing clear:
Though you are silent, what you say is true.

"There may have been the devil in my feet,
For down I blundered, like a fugitive,
To find the old room in Eleventh Street.
God save us!—I came here again to live."

We rose at that, and all the ghosts rose then,
And followed us unseen to his old room.
No longer a good place for living men
We found it, and we shivered in the gloom.

The goods he took away from there were few,
And soon we found ourselves outside once more,
Where now the lamps along the Avenue
Bloomed white for miles above an iron floor.

"Now lead me to the newest of hotels,"
He said, "and let your spleen be undeceived:
This ruin is not myself, but some one else;
I haven't failed; I've merely not achieved."

Whether he knew or not, he laughed and dined
With more of an immune regardlessness
Of pits before him and of sands behind
Than many a child at forty would confess;

And after, when the bells in *Boris* rang
Their tumult at the Metropolitan,
He rocked himself, and I believe he sang.
"God lives," he crooned aloud, "and I'm the man!"

He was. And even though the creature spoiled
All prophecies, I cherish his acclaim.
Three weeks he fattened; and five years he toiled
In Yonkers,—and then sauntered into fame.

And he may go now to what streets he will—
Eleventh, or the last, and little care;
But he would find the old room very still
Of evenings, and the ghosts would all be there.

I doubt if he goes after them; I doubt
If many of them ever come to him.
His memories are like lamps, and they go out;
Or if they burn, they flicker and are dim.

A light of other gleams he has to-day
And adulations of applauding hosts;
A famous danger, but a safer way
Than growing old alone among the ghosts.

But we may still be glad that we were wrong:
He fooled us, and we'd shrivel to deny it;
Though sometimes when old echoes ring too long,
I wish the bells in *Boris* would be quiet.

THE UNFORGIVEN

When he, who is the unforgiven,
Beheld her first, he found her fair:
No promise ever dreamt in heaven
Could then have lured him anywhere
That would have been away from there;
And all his wits had lightly striven,
Foiled with her voice, and eyes, and hair.

There's nothing in the saints and sages
To meet the shafts her glances had,
Or such as hers have had for ages
To blind a man till he be glad,
And humble him till he be mad.
The story would have many pages,
And would be neither good nor bad.

And, having followed, you would find him
Where properly the play begins;
But look for no red light behind him—
No fumes of many-colored sins,
Fanned high by screaming violins.
God knows what good it was to blind him,
Or whether man or woman wins.

And by the same eternal token,
Who knows just how it will all end?—
This drama of hard words unspoken,
This fireside farce, without a friend
Or enemy to comprehend
What augurs when two lives are broken,
And fear finds nothing left to mend.

He stares in vain for what awaits him,
And sees in Love a coin to toss;
He smiles, and her cold hush berates him
Beneath his hard half of the cross;

They wonder why it ever was;
And she, the unforgiving, hates him
More for her lack than for her loss.

He feeds with pride his indecision,
And shrinks from what will not occur,
Bequeathing with infirm derision
His ashes to the days that were,
Before she made him prisoner;
And labors to retrieve the vision
That he must once have had of her.

He waits, and there awaits an ending,
And he knows neither what nor when;
But no magicians are attending
To make him see as he saw then,
And he will never find again
The face that once had been the rending
Of all his purpose among men.

He blames her not, nor does he chide her,
And she has nothing new to say;
If he were Bluebeard he could hide her,
But that's not written in the play,
And there will be no change to-day;
Although, to the serene outsider,
There still would seem to be a way.

VETERAN SIRENS

THE ghost of Ninon would be sorry now
To laugh at them, were she to see them here,
So brave and so alert for learning how
To fence with reason for another year.

Age offers a far comelier diadem
Than theirs; but anguish has no eye for grace,
When time's malicious mercy cautions them
To think a while of number and of space.

The burning hope, the worn expectancy,
The martyred humor, and the maimed allure,
Cry out for time to end his levity,
And age to soften its investiture;

But they, though others fade and are still fair,
Defy their fairness and are unsubdued;
Although they suffer, they may not forswear
The patient ardor of the unpursued.

Poor flesh, to fight the calendar so long;
Poor vanity, so quaint and yet so brave;
Poor folly, so deceived and yet so strong,
So far from Ninon and so near the grave.

SIEGE PERILOUS

Long warned of many terrors more severe
To scorch him than hell's engines could awaken,
He scanned again, too far to be so near,
The fearful seat no man had ever taken.

So many other men with older eyes
Than his to see with older sight behind them
Had known so long their one way to be wise,—
Was any other thing to do than mind them?

So many a blasting parallel had seared
Confusion on his faith,—could he but wonder
If he were mad and right, or if he feared
God's fury told in shafted flame and thunder?

There fell one day upon his eyes a light
Ethereal, and he heard no more men speaking;
He saw their shaken heads, but no long sight
Was his but for the end that he went seeking.

The end he sought was not the end; the crown
He won shall unto many still be given.
Moreover, there was reason here to frown:
No fury thundered, no flame fell from heaven.

ANOTHER DARK LADY

THINK not, because I wonder where you fled,
That I would lift a pin to see you there;
You may, for me, be prowling anywhere,
So long as you show not your little head:
No dark and evil story of the dead
Would leave you less pernicious or less fair—
Not even Lilith, with her famous hair;
And Lilith was the devil, I have read.

I cannot hate you, for I loved you then.
The woods were golden then. There was a road
Through beeches; and I said their smooth feet showed
Like yours. Truth must have heard me from afar,
For I shall never have to learn again
That yours are cloven as no beech's are.

THE VOICE OF AGE

SHE'D look upon us, if she could,
As hard as Rhadamanthus would;
Yet one may see,—who sees her face,
Her crown of silver and of lace,

Her mystical serene address
Of age alloyed with loveliness,—
That she would not annihilate
The frailest of things animate.

She has opinions of our ways,
And if we're not all mad, she says,—
If our ways are not wholly worse
Than others, for not being hers,—
There might somehow be found a few
Less insane things for us to do,
And we might have a little heed
Of what Belshazzar couldn't read.

She feels, with all our furniture,
Room yet for something more secure
Than our self-kindled aureoles
To guide our poor forgotten souls;
But when we have explained that grace
Dwells now in doing for the race,
She nods—as if she were relieved;
Almost as if she were deceived.

She frowns at much of what she hears,
And shakes her head, and has her fears;
Though none may know, by any chance,
What rose-leaf ashes of romance
Are faintly stirred by later days
That would be well enough, she says,
If only people were more wise,
And grown-up children used their eyes.

THE POOR RELATION

No longer torn by what she knows
And sees within the eyes of others,
Her doubts are when the daylight goes,
Her fears are for the few she bothers.
She tells them it is wholly wrong
Of her to stay alive so long;
And when she smiles her forehead shows
A crinkle that had been her mother's.

Beneath her beauty, blanched with pain,
And wistful yet for being cheated,
A child would seem to ask again
A question many times repeated;
But no rebellion has betrayed
Her wonder at what she has paid
For memories that have no stain,
For triumph born to be defeated.

To those who come for what she was—
The few left who know where to find her—
She clings, for they are all she has;
And she may smile when they remind her,
As heretofore, of what they know
Of roses that are still to blow
By ways where not so much as grass
Remains of what she sees behind her.

They stay a while, and having done
What penance or the past requires,
They go, and leave her there alone
To count her chimneys and her spires.
Her lip shakes when they go away,
And yet she would not have them stay;
She knows as well as anyone
That Pity, having played, soon tires.

But one friend always reappears,
A good ghost, not to be forsaken;
Whereat she laughs and has no fears
Of what a ghost may reawaken,
But welcomes, while she wears and mends
The poor relation's odds and ends,
Her truant from a tomb of years—
Her power of youth so early taken.

Poor laugh, more slender than her song
It seems; and there are none to hear it
With even the stopped ears of the strong
For breaking heart or broken spirit.
The friends who clamored for her place,
And would have scratched her for her face,
Have lost her laughter for so long
That none would care enough to fear it.

None live who need fear anything
From her, whose losses are their pleasure;
The plover with a wounded wing
Stays not the flight that others measure;
So there she waits, and while she lives,
And death forgets, and faith forgives,
Her memories go foraging
For bits of childhood song they treasure.

And like a giant harp that hums
On always, and is always blending
The coming of what never comes
With what has past and had an ending,
The City trembles, throbs, and pounds
Outside, and through a thousand sounds
The small intolerable drums
Of Time are like slow drops descending.

Bereft enough to shame a sage
And given little to long sighing,

With no illusion to assuage
The lonely changelessness of dying,—
Unsought, unthought-of, and unheard,
She sings and watches like a bird,
Safe in a comfortable cage
From which there will be no more flying.

LLEWELLYN AND THE TREE

Could he have made Priscilla share
  The paradise that he had planned,
Llewellyn would have loved his wife
  As well as any in the land.

Could he have made Priscilla cease
  To goad him for what God left out,
Llewellyn would have been as mild
  As any we have read about.

Could all have been as all was not,
  Llewellyn would have had no story;
He would have stayed a quiet man
  And gone his quiet way to glory.

But howsoever mild he was
  Priscilla was implacable;
And whatsoever timid hopes
  He built—she found them, and they fell.

And this went on, with intervals
  Of labored harmony between
Resounding discords, till at last
  Llewellyn turned—as will be seen.

Priscilla, warmer than her name,
  And shriller than the sound of saws,

Pursued Llewellyn once too far,
　　Not knowing quite the man he was.

The more she said, the fiercer clung
　　The stinging garment of his wrath;
And this was all before the day
　　When Time tossed roses in his path.

Before the roses ever came
　　Llewellyn had already risen.
The roses may have ruined him,
　　They may have kept him out of prison.

And she who brought them, being Fate,
　　Made roses do the work of spears,—
Though many made no more of her
　　Than civet, coral, rouge, and years.

You ask us what Llewellyn saw,
　　But why ask what may not be given?
To some will come a time when change
　　Itself is beauty, if not heaven.

One afternoon Priscilla spoke,
　　And her shrill history was done;
At any rate, she never spoke
　　Like that again to anyone.

One gold October afternoon
　　Great fury smote the silent air;
And then Llewellyn leapt and fled
　　Like one with hornets in his hair.

Llewellyn left us, and he said
　　Forever, leaving few to doubt him;
And so, through frost and clicking leaves,
　　The Tilbury way went on without him.

And slowly, through the Tilbury mist,
  The stillness of October gold
Went out like beauty from a face.
  Priscilla watched it, and grew old.

He fled, still clutching in his flight
  The roses that had been his fall;
The Scarlet One, as you surmise,
  Fled with him, coral, rouge, and all.

Priscilla, waiting, saw the change
  Of twenty slow October moons;
And then she vanished, in her turn
  To be forgotten, like old tunes.

So they were gone—all three of them,
  I should have said, and said no more,
Had not a face once on Broadway
  Been one that I had seen before.

The face and hands and hair were old,
  But neither time nor penury
Could quench within Llewellyn's eyes
  The shine of his one victory.

The roses, faded and gone by,
  Left ruin where they once had reigned;
But on the wreck, as on old shells,
  The color of the rose remained.

His fictive merchandise I bought
  For him to keep and show again,
Then led him slowly from the crush
  Of his cold-shouldered fellow men.

"And so, Llewellyn," I began—
  "Not so," he said; "not so at all:

I've tried the world, and found it good,
  For more than twenty years this fall.

"And what the world has left of me
  Will go now in a little while."
And what the world had left of him
  Was partly an unholy guile.

"That I have paid for being calm
  Is what you see, if you have eyes;
For let a man be calm too long,
  He pays for much before he dies.

"Be calm when you are growing old
  And you have nothing else to do;
Pour not the wine of life too thin
  If water means the death of you.

"You say I might have learned at home
  The truth in season to be strong?
Not so; I took the wine of life
  Too thin, and I was calm too long.

"Like others who are strong too late,
  For me there was no going back;
For I had found another speed,
  And I was on the other track.

"God knows how far I might have gone
  Or what there might have been to see;
But my speed had a sudden end,
  And here you have the end of me."

The end or not, it may be now
  But little farther from the truth
To say those worn satiric eyes
  Had something of immortal youth.

He may among the millions here
  Be one; or he may, quite as well,
Be gone to find again the Tree
  Of Knowledge, out of which he fell.

He may be near us, dreaming yet
  Of unrepented rouge and coral;
Or in a grave without a name
  May be as far off as a moral.

BEWICK FINZER

TIME was when his half million drew
  The breath of six per cent;
But soon the worm of what-was-not
  Fed hard on his content;
And something crumbled in his brain
  When his half million went.

Time passed, and filled along with his
  The place of many more;
Time came, and hardly one of us
  Had credence to restore,
From what appeared one day, the man
  Whom we had known before.

The broken voice, the withered neck,
  The coat worn out with care,
The cleanliness of indigence,
  The brilliance of despair,
The fond imponderable dreams
  Of affluence,—all were there.

Poor Finzer, with his dreams and schemes,
  Fares hard now in the race,

With heart and eye that have a task
  When he looks in the face
Of one who might so easily
  Have been in Finzer's place.

He comes unfailing for the loan
  We give and then forget;
He comes, and probably for years
  Will he be coming yet,—
Familiar as an old mistake,
  And futile as regret.

BOKARDO

WELL, Bokardo, here we are;
  Make yourself at home.
Look around—you haven't far
  To look—and why be dumb?
Not the place that used to be,
Not so many things to see;
But there's room for you and me.
  And you—you've come.

Talk a little; or, if not,
  Show me with a sign
Why it was that you forgot
  What was yours and mine.
Friends, I gather, are small things
In an age when coins are kings;
Even at that, one hardly flings
  Friends before swine.

Rather strong? I knew as much,
  For it made you speak.
No offense to swine, as such,
  But why this hide-and-seek?

You have something on your side,
And you wish you might have died,
So you tell me. And you tried
   One night last week?

You tried hard? And even then
   Found a time to pause?
When you try as hard again,
   You'll have another cause.
When you find yourself at odds
With all dreamers of all gods,
You may smite yourself with rods—
   But not the laws.

Though they seem to show a spite
   Rather devilish,
They move on as with a might
   Stronger than your wish.
Still, however strong they be,
They bide man's authority:
Xerxes, when he flogged the sea,
   May've scared a fish.

It's a comfort, if you like,
   To keep honor warm,
But as often as you strike
   The laws, you do no harm.
To the laws, I mean. To you—
That's another point of view,
One you may as well indue
   With some alarm.

Not the most heroic face
   To present, I grant;
Nor will you insure disgrace
   By fearing what you want.
Freedom has a world of sides,
And if reason once derides

Courage, then your courage hides
    A deal of cant.

Learn a little to forget
    Life was once a feast;
You aren't fit for dying yet,
    So don't be a beast.
Few men with a mind will say,
Thinking twice, that they can pay
Half their debts of yesterday,
    Or be released.

There's a debt now on your mind
    More than any gold?
And there's nothing you can find
    Out there in the cold?
Only—what's his name?—Remorse?
And Death riding on his horse?
Well, be glad there's nothing worse
    Than you have told.

Leave Remorse to warm his hands
    Outside in the rain.
As for Death, he understands,
    And he will come again.
Therefore, till your wits are clear,
Flourish and be quiet—here.
But a devil at each ear
    Will be a strain?

Past a doubt they will indeed,
    More than you have earned.
I say that because you need
    Ablution, being burned?
Well, if you must have it so,
Your last flight went rather low.
Better say you had to know
    What you have learned.

146

And that's over. Here you are,
   Battered by the past.
Time will have his little scar,
   But the wound won't last.
Nor shall harrowing surprise
Find a world without its eyes
If a star fades when the skies
   Are overcast.

God knows there are lives enough,
   Crushed, and too far gone
Longer to make sermons of,
   And those we leave alone.
Others, if they will, may rend
The worn patience of a friend
Who, though smiling, sees the end,
   With nothing done.

But your fervor to be free
   Fled the faith it scorned;
Death demands a decency
   Of you, and you are warned.
But for all we give we get
Mostly blows? Don't be upset;
You, Bokardo, are not yet
   Consumed or mourned.

There'll be falling into view
   Much to rearrange;
And there'll be a time for you
   To marvel at the change.
They that have the least to fear
Question hardest what is here;
When long-hidden skies are clear,
   The stars look strange.

THE MAN AGAINST THE SKY

BETWEEN me and the sunset, like a dome
Against the glory of a world on fire,
Now burned a sudden hill,
Bleak, round, and high, by flame-lit height made higher,
With nothing on it for the flame to kill
Save one who moved and was alone up there
To loom before the chaos and the glare
As if he were the last god going home
Unto his last desire.

Dark, marvelous, and inscrutable he moved on
Till down the fiery distance he was gone,
Like one of those eternal, remote things
That range across a man's imaginings
When a sure music fills him and he knows
What he may say thereafter to few men,—
The touch of ages having wrought
An echo and a glimpse of what he thought
A phantom or a legend until then;
For whether lighted over ways that save,
Or lured from all repose,
If he go on too far to find a grave,
Mostly alone he goes.

Even he, who stood where I had found him,
On high with fire all round him,
Who moved along the molten west,
And over the round hill's crest
That seemed half ready with him to go down,
Flame-bitten and flame-cleft,
As if there were to be no last thing left
Of a nameless unimaginable town,—
Even he who climbed and vanished may have taken
Down to the perils of a depth not known,
From death defended though by men forsaken,

The bread that every man must eat alone;
He may have walked while others hardly dared
Look on to see him stand where many fell;
And upward out of that, as out of hell,
He may have sung and striven
To mount where more of him shall yet be given,
Bereft of all retreat,
To sevenfold heat,—
As on a day when three in Dura shared
The furnace, and were spared
For glory by that king of Babylon
Who made himself so great that God, who heard,
Covered him with long feathers, like a bird.

Again, he may have gone down easily,
By comfortable altitudes, and found,
As always, underneath him solid ground
Whereon to be sufficient and to stand
Possessed already of the promised land,
Far stretched and fair to see:
A good sight, verily,
And one to make the eyes of her who bore him
Shine glad with hidden tears.
Why question of his ease of who before him,
In one place or another where they left
Their names as far behind them as their bones,
And yet by dint of slaughter toil and theft,
And shrewdly sharpened stones,
Carved hard the way for his ascendency
Through deserts of lost years?
Why trouble him now who sees and hears
No more than what his innocence requires,
And therefore to no other height aspires
Than one at which he neither quails nor tires?
He may do more by seeing what he sees
Than others eager for iniquities;
He may, by seeing all things for the best,
Incite futurity to do the rest.

Or with an even likelihood,
He may have met with atrabilious eyes
The fires of time on equal terms and passed
Indifferently down, until at last
His only kind of grandeur would have been,
Apparently, in being seen.
He may have had for evil or for good
No argument; he may have had no care
For what without himself went anywhere
To failure or to glory, and least of all
For such a stale, flamboyant miracle;
He may have been the prophet of an art
Immovable to old idolatries;
He may have been a player without a part,
Annoyed that even the sun should have the skies
For such a flaming way to advertise;
He may have been a painter sick at heart
With Nature's toiling for a new surprise;
He may have been a cynic, who now, for all
Of anything divine that his effete
Negation may have tasted,
Saw truth in his own image, rather small,
Forbore to fever the ephemeral,
Found any barren height a good retreat
From any swarming street,
And in the sun saw power superbly wasted;
And when the primitive old-fashioned stars
Came out again to shine on joys and wars
More primitive, and all arrayed for doom,
He may have proved a world a sorry thing
In his imagining,
And life a lighted highway to the tomb.

Or, mounting with infirm unsearching tread,
His hopes to chaos led,
He may have stumbled up there from the past,
And with an aching strangeness viewed the last
Abysmal conflagration of his dreams,—

A flame where nothing seems
To burn but flame itself, by nothing fed;
And while it all went out,
Not even the faint anodyne of doubt
May then have eased a painful going down
From pictured heights of power and lost renown,
Revealed at length to his outlived endeavor
Remote and unapproachable forever;
And at his heart there may have gnawed
Sick memories of a dead faith foiled and flawed
And long dishonored by the living death
Assigned alike by chance
To brutes and hierophants;
And anguish fallen on those he loved around him
May once have dealt the last blow to confound him
And so have left him as death leaves a child,
Who sees it all too near;
And he who knows no young way to forget
May struggle to the tomb unreconciled.
Whatever suns may rise or set
There may be nothing kinder for him here
Than shafts and agonies;
And under these
He may cry out and stay on horribly;
Or, seeing in death too small a thing to fear,
He may go forward like a stoic Roman
Where pangs and terrors in his pathway lie,—
Or, seizing the swift logic of a woman,
Curse God and die.

Or maybe there, like many another one
Who might have stood aloft and looked ahead,
Black-dawn against wild red,
He may have built, unawed by fiery gules
That in him no commotion stirred,
A living reason out of molecules
Why molecules occurred,
And one for smiling when he might have sighed

Had he seen far enough,
And in the same inevitable stuff
Discovered an odd reason too for pride
In being what he must have been by laws
Infrangible and for no kind of cause.
Deterred by no confusion or surprise
He may have seen with his mechanic eyes
A world without a meaning, and had room,
Alone amid magnificence and doom,
To build himself an airy monument
That should, or fail him in his vague intent,
Outlast an accidental universe—
To call it nothing worse—
Or, by the burrowing guile
Of Time disintegrated and effaced,
Like once-remembered mighty trees go down
To ruin, of which by man may now be traced
No part sufficient even to be rotten,
And in the book of things that are forgotten
Is entered as a thing not quite worth while.
He may have been so great
That satraps would have shivered at his frown.
And all he prized alive may rule a state
No larger than a grave that holds a clown;
He may have been a master of his fate,
And of his atoms,—ready as another
In his emergence to exonerate
His father and his mother;
He may have been a captain of a host,
Self-eloquent and ripe for prodigies,
Doomed here to swell by dangerous degrees,
And then give up the ghost.
Nahum's great grasshoppers were such as these,
Sun-scattered and soon lost.

Whatever the dark road he may have taken,
This man who stood on high
And faced alone the sky,

Whatever drove or lured or guided him,—
A vision answering a faith unshaken,
An easy trust assumed of easy trials,
A sick negation born of weak denials,
A crazed abhorrence of an old condition,
A blind attendance on a brief ambition,—
Whatever stayed him or derided him,
His way was even as ours;
And we, with all our wounds and all our powers,
Must each await alone at his own height
Another darkness or another light;
And there, of our poor self dominion reft,
If inference and reason shun
Hell, Heaven, and Oblivion,
May thwarted will (perforce precarious,
But for our conservation better thus)
Have no misgiving left
Of doing yet what here we leave undone?
Or if unto the last of these we cleave,
Believing or protesting we believe
In such an idle and ephemeral
Florescence of the diabolical,—
If, robbed of two fond old enormities,
Our being had no onward auguries,
What then were this great love of ours to say
For launching other lives to voyage again
A little farther into time and pain,
A little faster in a futile chase
For a kingdom and a power and a Race
That would have still in sight
A manifest end of ashes and eternal night?
Is this the music of the toys we shake
So loud,—as if there might be no mistake
Somewhere in our indomitable will?
Are we no greater than the noise we make
Along one blind atomic pilgrimage
Whereon by crass chance billeted we go
Because our brains and bones and cartilage

Will have it so?
If this we say, then let us all be still
About our share in it, and live and die
More quietly thereby.

Where was he going, this man against the sky?
You know not, nor do I.
But this we know, if we know anything:
That we may laugh and fight and sing
And of our transience here make offering
To an orient Word that will not be erased,
Or, save in incommunicable gleams
Too permanent for dreams,
Be found or known.
No tonic and ambitious irritant
Of increase or of want
Has made an otherwise insensate waste
Of ages overthrown
A ruthless, veiled, implacable foretaste
Of other ages that are still to be
Depleted and rewarded variously
Because a few, by fate's economy,
Shall seem to move the world the way it goes;
No soft evangel of equality,
Safe-cradled in a communal repose
That huddles into death and may at last
Be covered well with equatorial snows—
And all for what, the devil only knows—
Will aggregate an inkling to confirm
The credit of a sage or of a worm,
Or tell us why one man in five
Should have a care to stay alive
While in his heart he feels no violence
Laid on his humor and intelligence
When infant Science makes a pleasant face
And waves again that hollow toy, the Race;
No planetary trap where souls are wrought
For nothing but the sake of being caught

And sent again to nothing will attune
Itself to any key of any reason
Why man should hunger through another season
To find out why 'twere better late than soon
To go away and let the sun and moon
And all the silly stars illuminate
A place for creeping things,
And those that root and trumpet and have wings,
And herd and ruminate,
Or dive and flash and poise in rivers and seas,
Or by their loyal tails in lofty trees
Hang screeching lewd victorious derision
Of man's immortal vision.

Shall we, because Eternity records
Too vast an answer for the time-born words
We spell, whereof so many are dead that once
In our capricious lexicons
Were so alive and final, hear no more
The Word itself, the living word
That none alive has ever heard
Or ever spelt,
And few have ever felt
Without the fears and old surrenderings
And terrors that began
When Death let fall a feather from his wings
And humbled the first man?
Because the weight of our humility,
Wherefrom we gain
A little wisdom and much pain,
Falls here too sore and there too tedious,
Are we in anguish or complacency,
Not looking far enough ahead
To see by what mad couriers we are led
Along the roads of the ridiculous,
To pity ourselves and laugh at faith
And while we curse life bear it?
And if we see the soul's dead end in death,

Are we to fear it?
What folly is here that has not yet a name
Unless we say outright that we are liars?
What have we seen beyond our sunset fires
That lights again the way by which we came?
Why pay we such a price, and one we give
So clamoringly, for each racked empty day
That leads one more last human hope away,
As quiet fiends would lead past our crazed eyes
Our children to an unseen sacrifice?
If after all that we have lived and thought,
All comes to Nought,—
If there be nothing after Now,
And we be nothing anyhow,
And we know that,—why live?
'Twere sure but weaklings' vain distress
To suffer dungeons where so many doors
Will open on the cold eternal shores
That look sheer down
To the dark tideless floods of Nothingness
Where all who know may drown.

From

THE THREE

TAVERNS

1920

———◆●◆———

To

Thomas Sergeant Perry

and

Lilla Cabot Perry

THE VALLEY OF THE SHADOW

THERE were faces to remember in the Valley of the Shadow,
There were faces unregarded, there were faces to forget;
There were fires of grief and fear that are a few forgotten ashes,
There were sparks of recognition that are not forgotten yet.
For at first, with an amazed and overwhelming indignation
At a measureless malfeasance that obscurely willed it thus,
They were lost and unacquainted—till they found themselves in
others,
Who had groped as they were groping where dim ways were
perilous.

There were lives that were as dark as are the fears and intuitions
Of a child who knows himself and is alone with what he knows;
There were pensioners of dreams and there were debtors of illusions,
All to fail before the triumph of a weed that only grows.
There were thirsting heirs of golden sieves that held not wine or
water,
And had no names in traffic or more value there than toys:
There were blighted sons of wonder in the Valley of the Shadow,
Where they suffered and still wondered why their wonder made
no noise.

There were slaves who dragged the shackles of a precedent
unbroken,
Demonstrating the fulfilment of unalterable schemes,
Which had been, before the cradle, Time's inexorable tenants
Of what were now the dusty ruins of their father's dreams.
There were these, and there were many who had stumbled up to
manhood,
Where they saw too late. the road they should have taken long ago:
There were thwarted clerks and fiddlers in the Valley of the
Shadow,
The commemorative wreckage of what others did not know.

And there were daughters older than the mothers who had borne
them,

Being older in their wisdom, which is older than the earth;
And they were going forward only farther into darkness,
Unrelieved as were the blasting obligations of their birth;
And among them, giving always what was not for their possession,
There were maidens, very quiet, with no quiet in their eyes;
There were daughters of the silence in the Valley of the Shadow,
Each an isolated item in the family sacrifice.

There were creepers among catacombs where dull regrets were
    torches,
Giving light enough to show them what was there upon the shelves—
Where there was more for them to see than pleasure would
    remember
Of something that had been alive and once had been themselves.
There were some who stirred the ruins with a solid imprecation,
While as many fled repentance for the promise of despair:
There were drinkers of wrong waters in the Valley of the Shadow,
And all the sparkling ways were dust that once had led them there.

There were some who knew the steps of Age incredibly beside them,
And his fingers upon shoulders that had never felt the wheel;
And their last of empty trophies was a gilded cup of nothing,
Which a contemplating vagabond would not have come to steal.
Long and often had they figured for a larger valuation,
But the size of their addition was the balance of a doubt:
There were gentlemen of leisure in the Valley of the Shadow,
Not allured by retrospection, disenchanted, and played out.

And among the dark endurances of unavowed reprisals
There were silent eyes of envy that saw little but saw well;
And over beauty's aftermath of hazardous ambitions
There were tears for what had vanished as they vanished where
    they fell.
Not assured of what was theirs, and always hungry for the nameless,
There were some whose only passion was for Time who made them
    cold:
There were numerous fair women in the Valley of the Shadow,
Dreaming rather less of heaven than of hell when they were old.

Now and then, as if to scorn the common touch of common sorrow,
There were some who gave a few the distant pity of a smile;
And another cloaked a soul as with an ash of human embers,
Having covered thus a treasure that would last him for a while.
There were many by the presence of the many disaffected,
Whose exemption was included in the weight that others bore:
There were seekers after darkness in the Valley of the Shadow,
And they alone were there to find what they were looking for.

So they were, and so they are; and as they came are coming others,
And among them are the fearless and the meek and the unborn;
And a question that has held us heretofore without an answer
May abide without an answer until all have ceased to mourn.
For the children of the dark are more to name than are the wretched,
Or the broken, or the weary, or the baffled, or the shamed:
There are builders of new mansions in the Valley of the Shadow,
And among them are the dying and the blinded and the maimed.

THE WANDERING JEW

I SAW by looking in his eyes
That they remembered everything;
And this was how I came to know
That he was here, still wandering.
For though the figure and the scene
Were never to be reconciled,
I knew the man as I had known
His image when I was a child.

With evidence at every turn,
I should have held it safe to guess
That all the newness of New York
Had nothing new in loneliness;
Yet here was one who might be Noah,
Or Nathan, or Abimelech,

Or Lamech, out of ages lost,—
Or, more than all, Melchizedek.

Assured that he was none of these,
I gave them back their names again,
To scan once more those endless eyes
Where all my questions ended then.
I found in them what they revealed
That I shall not live to forget,
And wondered if they found in mine
Compassion that I might regret.

Pity, I learned, was not the least
Of time's offending benefits
That had now for so long impugned
The conservation of his wits:
Rather it was that I should yield,
Alone, the fealty that presents
The tribute of a tempered ear
To an untempered eloquence.

Before I pondered long enough
On whence he came and who he was,
I trembled at his ringing wealth
Of manifold anathemas;
I wondered, while he seared the world,
What new defection ailed the race,
And if it mattered how remote
Our fathers were from such a place,

Before there was an hour for me
To contemplate with less concern
The crumbling realm awaiting us
Than his that was beyond return,
A dawning on the dust of years
Had shaped with an elusive light
Mirages of remembered scenes
That were no longer for the sight.

For now the gloom that hid the man
Became a daylight on his wrath,
And one wherein my fancy viewed
New lions ramping in his path.
The old were dead and had no fangs,
Wherefore he loved them—seeing not
They were the same that in their time
Had eaten everything they caught.

The world around him was a gift
Of anguish to his eyes and ears,
And one that he had long reviled
As fit for devils, not for seers.
Where, then, was there a place for him
That on this other side of death
Saw nothing good, as he had seen
No good come out of Nazareth?

Yet here there was a reticence,
And I believe his only one,
That hushed him as if he beheld
A Presence that would not be gone.
In such a silence he confessed
How much there was to be denied;
And he would look at me and live,
As others might have looked and died.

As if at last he knew again
That he had always known, his eyes
Were like to those of one who gazed
On those of One who never dies.
For such a moment he revealed
What life has in it to be lost;
And I could ask if what I saw,
Before me there, was man or ghost.

He may have died so many times
That all there was of him to see

Was pride, that kept itself alive
As too rebellious to be free;
He may have told, when more than once
Humility seemed imminent,
How many a lonely time in vain
The Second Coming came and went.

Whether he still defies or not
The failure of an angry task
That relegates him out of time
To chaos, I can only ask.
But as I knew him, so he was;
And somewhere among men to-day
Those old, unyielding eyes may flash,
And flinch—and look the other way.

THE MILL

THE miller's wife had waited long,
  The tea was cold, the fire was dead;
And there might yet be nothing wrong
  In how he went and what he said:
"There are no millers any more,"
  Was all that she had heard him say;
And he had lingered at the door
  So long that it seemed yesterday.

Sick with a fear that had no form
  She knew that she was there at last;
And in the mill there was a warm
  And mealy fragrance of the past.
What else there was would only seem
  To say again what he had meant;
And what was hanging from a beam
  Would not have heeded where she went.

And if she thought it followed her,
    She may have reasoned in the dark
That one way of the few there were
    Would hide her and would leave no mark:
Black water, smooth above the weir
    Like starry velvet in the night,
Though ruffled once, would soon appear
    The same as ever to the sight.

THE DARK HILLS

DARK hills at evening in the west,
Where sunset hovers like a sound
Of golden horns that sang to rest
Old bones of warriors under ground,
Far now from all the bannered ways
Where flash the legions of the sun,
You fade—as if the last of days
Were fading, and all wars were done.

DEMOS

I

ALL you that are enamored of my name
    And least intent on what most I require,
    Beware; for my design and your desire,
Deplorably, are not as yet the same.
Beware, I say, the failure and the shame
    Of losing that for which you now aspire
    So blindly, and of hazarding entire
The gift that I was bringing when I came.

Give as I will, I cannot give you sight
    Whereby to see that with you there are some
    To lead you, and be led. But they are dumb
Before the wrangling and the shrill delight
    Of your deliverance that has not come,
And shall not, if I fail you—as I might.

II

So little have you seen of what awaits
    Your fevered glimpse of a democracy
    Confused and foiled with an equality
Not equal to the envy it creates,
That you see not how near you are the gates
    Of an old king who listens fearfully
    To you that are outside and are to be
The noisy lords of imminent estates.

Rather be then your prayer that you shall have
    Your kingdom undishonored. Having all,
    See not the great among you for the small,
But hear their silence; for the few shall save
    The many, or the many are to fall—
Still to be wrangling in a noisy grave.

THE FLYING DUTCHMAN

Unyielding in the pride of his defiance,
    Afloat with none to serve or to command,
Lord of himself at last, and all by Science,
    He seeks the Vanished Land.

Alone, by the one light of his one thought,
    He steers to find the shore from which we came,
Fearless of in what coil he may be caught
    On seas that have no name.

166

Into the night he sails; and after night
    There is a dawning, though there be no sun;
Wherefore, with nothing but himself in sight,
    Unsighted, he sails on.

At last there is a lifting of the cloud
    Between the flood before him and the sky;
And then—though he may curse the Power aloud
    That has no power to die—

He steers himself away from what is haunted
    By the old ghost of what has been before,—
Abandoning, as always, and undaunted,
    One fog-walled island more.

TACT

Observant of the way she told
    So much of what was true,
No vanity could long withhold
    Regard that was her due:
She spared him the familiar guile,
    So easily achieved,
That only made a man to smile
    And left him undeceived.

Aware that all imagining
    Of more than what she meant
Would urge an end of everything,
    He stayed; and when he went,
They parted with a merry word
    That was to him as light
As any that was ever heard
    Upon a starry night.

167

She smiled a little, knowing well
    That he would not remark
The ruins of a day that fell
    Around her in the dark:
He saw no ruins anywhere,
    Nor fancied there were scars
On anyone who lingered there,
    Alone below the stars.

TASKER NORCROSS

"WHETHER all towns and all who live in them—
So long as they be somewhere in this world
That we in our complacency call ours—
Are more or less the same, I leave to you.
I should say less. Whether or not, meanwhile,
We've all two legs—and as for that, we haven't—
There were three kinds of men where I was born:
The good, the not so good, and Tasker Norcross.
Now there are two kinds."

                    "Meaning, as I divine,
Your friend is dead," I ventured.

                            Ferguson,
Who talked himself at last out of the world
He censured, and is therefore silent now,
Agreed indifferently: "My friends are dead—
Or most of them."

                    "Remember one that isn't,"
I said, protesting. "Honor him for his ears;
Treasure him also for his understanding."
Ferguson sighed, and then talked on again:
"You have an overgrown alacrity

For saying nothing much and hearing less;
And I've a thankless wonder, at the start,
How much it is to you that I shall tell
What I have now to say of Tasker Norcross,
And how much to the air that is around you.
But given a patience that is not averse
To the slow tragedies of haunted men—
Horrors, in fact, if you've a skilful eye
To know them at their firesides, or out walking,—"

"Horrors," I said, "are my necessity;
And I would have them, for their best effect,
Always out walking."

                Ferguson frowned at me:
"The wisest of us are not those who laugh
Before they know. Most of us never know—
Or the long toil of our mortality
Would not be done. Most of us never know—
And there you have a reason to believe
In God, if you may have no other. Norcross,
Or so I gather of his infirmity,
Was given to know more than he should have known,
And only God knows why. See for yourself
An old house full of ghosts of ancestors,
Who did their best, or worst, and having done it,
Died honorably; and each with a distinction
That hardly would have been for him that had it,
Had honor failed him wholly as a friend.
Honor that is a friend begets a friend.

Whether or not we love him, still we have him;
And we must live somehow by what we have,
Or then we die. If you say chemistry,
Then you must have your molecules in motion,
And in their right abundance. Failing either,
You have not long to dance. Failing a friend,
A genius, or a madness, or a faith

Larger than desperation, you are here
For as much longer than you like as may be.
Imagining now, by way of an example,
Myself a more or less remembered phantom—
Again, I should say less—how many times
A day should I come back to you? No answer.
Forgive me when I seem a little careless,
But we must have examples, or be lucid
Without them; and I question your adherence
To such an undramatic narrative
As this of mine, without the personal hook."

"A time is given in Ecclesiastes
For divers works," I told him. "Is there one
For saying nothing in return for nothing?
If not, there should be." I could feel his eyes,
And they were like two cold inquiring points
Of a sharp metal. When I looked again,
To see them shine, the cold that I had felt
Was gone to make way for a smouldering
Of lonely fire that I, as I knew then,
Could never quench with kindness or with lies.
I should have done whatever there was to do
For Ferguson, yet I could not have mourned
In honesty for once around the clock
The loss of him, for my sake or for his,
Try as I might; nor would his ghost approve,
Had I the power and the unthinking will
To make him tread again without an aim
The road that was behind him—and without
The faith, or friend, or genius, or the madness
That he contended was imperative.

After a silence that had been too long,
"It may be quite as well we don't," he said;
"As well, I mean, that we don't always say it.
You know best what I mean, and I suppose
You might have said it better. What was that?

Incorrigible? Am I incorrigible?
Well, it's a word; and a word has its use,
Or, like a man, it will soon have a grave.
It's a good word enough. Incorrigible,
May be, for all I know, the word for Norcross.
See for yourself that house of his again
That he called home: An old house, painted white,
Square as a box, and chillier than a tomb
To look at or to live in. There were trees—
Too many of them, if such a thing may be—
Before it and around it. Down in front
There was a road, a railroad, and a river;
Then there were hills behind it, and more trees.
The thing would fairly stare at you through trees,
Like a pale inmate out of a barred window
With a green shade half down; and I dare say
People who passed have said: 'There's where he lives.
We know him, but we do not seem to know
That we remember any good of him,
Or any evil that is interesting.
There you have all we know and all we care.'
They might have said it in all sorts of ways;
And then, if they perceived a cat, they might
Or might not have remembered what they said.
The cat might have a personality—
And maybe the same one the Lord left out
Of Tasker Norcross, who, for lack of it,
Saw the same sun go down year after year;
All which at last was my discovery.
And only mine, so far as evidence
Enlightens one more darkness. You have known
All round you, all your days, men who are nothing—
Nothing, I mean, so far as time tells yet
Of any other need it has of them
Than to make sextons hardy—but no less
Are to themselves incalculably something,
And therefore to be cherished. God, you see,
Being sorry for them in their fashioning,

Indemnified them with a quaint esteem
Of self, and with illusions long as life.
You know them well, and you have smiled at them;
And they, in their serenity, may have had
Their time to smile at you. Blessed are they
That see themselves for what they never were
Or were to be, and are, for their defect,
At ease with mirrors and the dim remarks
That pass their tranquil ears."

                              "Come, come," said I;
"There may be names in your compendium
That we are not yet all on fire for shouting.
Skin most of us of our mediocrity,
We should have nothing then that we could scratch.
The picture smarts. Cover it, if you please,
And do so rather gently. Now for Norcross."

Ferguson closed his eyes in resignation,
While a dead sigh came out of him. "Good God!"
He said, and said it only half aloud,
As if he knew no longer now, nor cared,
If one were there to listen: "Have I said nothing—
Nothing at all—of Norcross? Do you mean
To patronize him till his name becomes
A toy made out of letters? If a name
Is all you need, arrange an honest column
Of all the people you have ever known
That you have never liked. You'll have enough;
And you'll have mine, moreover. No, not yet.
If I assume too many privileges,
I pay, and I alone, for their assumption;
By which, if I assume a darker knowledge
Of Norcross than another, let the weight
Of my injustice aggravate the load
That is not on your shoulders. When I came
To know this fellow Norcross in his house,
I found him as I found him in the street—

No more, no less; indifferent, but no better.
'Worse' were not quite the word: he was not bad;
He was not . . . well, he was not anything.
Has your invention ever entertained
The picture of a dusty worm so dry
That even the early bird would shake his head
And fly on farther for another breakfast?"

"But why forget the fortune of the worm,"
I said, "if in the dryness you deplore
Salvation centred and endured? Your Norcross
May have been one for many to have envied."

"Salvation? Fortune? Would the worm say that?
He might; and therefore I dismiss the worm
With all dry things but one. Figures away,
Do you begin to see this man a little?
Do you begin to see him in the air,
With all the vacant horrors of his outline
For you to fill with more than it will hold?
If so, you needn't crown yourself at once
With epic laurel if you seem to fill it.
Horrors, I say, for in the fires and forks
Of a new hell—if one were not enough—
I doubt if a new horror would have held him
With a malignant ingenuity
More to be feared than his before he died.
You smile, as if in doubt. Well, smile again.
Now come into his house, along with me:
The four square sombre things that you see first
Around you are four walls that go as high
As to the ceiling. Norcross knew them well,
And he knew others like them. Fasten to that
With all the claws of your intelligence;
And hold the man before you in his house
As if he were a white rat in a box,
And one that knew himself to be no other.
I tell you twice that he knew all about it,

That you may not forget the worst of all
Our tragedies begin with what we know.
Could Norcross only not have known, I wonder
How many would have blessed and envied him!
Could he have had the usual eye for spots
On others, and for none upon himself,
I smile to ponder on the carriages
That might as well as not have clogged the town
In honor of his end. For there was gold,
You see, though all he needed was a little,
And what he gave said nothing of who gave it.
He would have given it all if in return
There might have been a more sufficient face
To greet him when he shaved. Though you insist
It is the dower, and always, of our degree
Not to be cursed with such invidious insight,
Remember that you stand, you and your fancy,
Now in his house; and since we are together,
See for yourself and tell me what you see.
Tell me the best you see. Make a slight noise
Of recognition when you find a book
That you would not as lief read upside down
As otherwise, for example. If there you fail,
Observe the walls and lead me to the place,
Where you are led. If there you meet a picture
That holds you near it for a longer time
Than you are sorry, you may call it yours,
And hang it in the dark of your remembrance,
Where Norcross never sees. How can he see
That has no eyes to see? And as for music,
He paid with empty wonder for the pangs
Of his infrequent forced endurance of it;
And having had no pleasure, paid no more
For needless immolation, or for the sight
Of those who heard what he was never to hear.
To see them listening was itself enough
To make him suffer; and to watch worn eyes,
On other days, of strangers who forgot

Their sorrows and their failures and themselves
Before a few mysterious odds and ends
Of marble carted from the Parthenon—
And all for seeing what he was never to see,
Because it was alive and he was dead—
Here was a wonder that was more profound
Than any that was in fiddles and brass horns.

"He knew, and in his knowledge there was death.
He knew there was a region all around him
That lay outside man's havoc and affairs,
And yet was not all hostile to their tumult,
Where poets would have served and honored him,
And saved him, had there been anything to save.
But there was nothing, and his tethered range
Was only a small desert. Kings of song
Are not for thrones in deserts. Towers of sound
And flowers of sense are but a waste of heaven
Where there is none to know them from the rocks
And sand-grass of his own monotony
That makes earth less than earth. He could see that,
And he could see no more. The captured light
That may have been or not, for all he cared,
The song that is in sculpture was not his,
But only, to his God-forgotten eyes,
One more immortal nonsense in a world
Where all was mortal, or had best be so,
And so be done with. 'Art,' he would have said,
'Is not life, and must therefore be a lie;'
And with a few profundities like that
He would have controverted and dismissed
The benefit of the Greeks. He had heard of them,
As he had heard of his aspiring soul—
Never to the perceptible advantage,
In his esteem, of either. 'Faith,' he said,
Or would have said if he had thought of it,
'Lives in the same house with Philosophy,
Where the two feed on scraps and are forlorn

175

As orphans after war.' He could see stars,
On a clear night, but he had not an eye
To see beyond them. He could hear spoken words,
But had no ear for silence when alone.
He could eat food of which he knew the savor,
But had no palate for the Bread of Life,
That human desperation, to his thinking,
Made famous long ago, having no other.
Now do you see? Do you begin to see?"

I told him that I did begin to see;
And I was nearer than I should have been
To laughing at his malign inclusiveness,
When I considered that, with all our speed,
We are not laughing yet at funerals.
I see him now as I could see him then,
And I see now that it was good for me,
As it was good for him, that I was quiet;
For Time's eye was on Ferguson, and the shaft
Of its inquiring hesitancy had touched him,
Or so I chose to fancy more than once
Before he told of Norcross. When the word
Of his release (he would have called it so)
Made half an inch of news, there were no tears
That are recorded. Women there may have been
To wish him back, though I should say, not knowing,
The few there were to mourn were not for love,
And were not lovely. Nothing of them, at least,
Was in the meagre legend that I gathered
Years after, when a chance of travel took me
So near the region of his nativity
That a few miles of leisure brought me there;
For there I found a friendly citizen
Who led me to his house among the trees
That were above a railroad and a river.
Square as a box and chillier than a tomb
It was indeed, to look at or to live in—
All which had I been told. "Ferguson died,"

The stranger said, "and then there was an auction.
I live here, but I've never yet been warm.
Remember him? Yes, I remember him.
I knew him—as a man may know a tree—
For twenty years. He may have held himself
A little high when he was here, but now . . .
Yes, I remember Ferguson. Oh, yes."
Others, I found, remembered Ferguson,
But none of them had heard of Tasker Norcross.

A SONG AT SHANNON'S

Two men came out of Shannon's, having known
The faces of each other for as long
As they had listened there to an old song,
Sung thinly in a wastrel monotone
By some unhappy night-bird, who had flown
Too many times and with a wing too strong
To save himself, and so done heavy wrong
To more frail elements than his alone.

Slowly away they went, leaving behind
More light than was before them. Neither met
The other's eyes again or said a word.
Each to his loneliness or to his kind,
Went his own way, and with his own regret,
Not knowing what the other may have heard.

SOUVENIR

A VANISHED house that for an hour I knew
By some forgotten chance when I was young
Had once a glimmering window overhung
With honeysuckle wet with evening dew.
Along the path tall dusky dahlias grew,
And shadowy hydrangeas reached and swung
Ferociously; and over me, among
The moths and mysteries, a blurred bat flew.

Somewhere within there were dim presences
Of days that hovered and of years gone by.
I waited, and between their silences
There was an evanescent faded noise;
And though a child, I knew it was the voice
Of one whose occupation was to die.

FIRELIGHT

TEN years together without yet a cloud,
They seek each other's eyes at intervals
Of gratefulness to firelight and four walls
For love's obliteration of the crowd.
Serenely and perennially endowed
And bowered as few may be, their joy recalls
No snake, no sword; and over them there falls
The blessing of what neither says aloud.

Wiser for silence, they were not so glad
Were she to read the graven tale of lines
On the wan face of one somewhere alone;
Nor were they more content could he have had
Her thoughts a moment since of one who shines
Apart, and would be hers if he had known.

THE RAT

As often as he let himself be seen
We pitied him, or scorned him, or deplored
The inscrutable profusion of the Lord
Who shaped as one of us a thing so mean—
Who made him human when he might have been
A rat, and so been wholly in accord
With any other creature we abhorred
As always useless and not always clean.

Now he is hiding all alone somewhere,
And in a final hole not ready then;
For now he is among those over there
Who are not coming back to us again.
And we who do the fiction of our share
Say less of rats and rather more of men.

RAHEL TO VARNHAGEN

NOTE.—Rahel Robert and Varnhagen von Ense were married,
after many protestations on her part, in 1814. The marriage—so
far as he was concerned at any rate—appears to have been satis-
factory.

Now you have read them all; or if not all,
As many as in all conscience I should fancy
To be enough. There are no more of them—
Or none to burn your sleep, or to bring dreams
Of devils. If these are not sufficient, surely
You are a strange young man. I might live on
Alone, and for another forty years,
Or not quite forty,—are you happier now?—
Always to ask if there prevailed elsewhere
Another like yourself that would have held
These aged hands as long as you have held them,
Not once observing, for all I can see,

How they are like your mother's. Well, you have read
His letters now, and you have heard me say
That in them are the cinders of a passion
That was my life; and you have not yet broken
Your way out of my house, out of my sight,—
Into the street. You are a strange young man.
I know as much as that of you, for certain;
And I'm already praying, for your sake,
That you be not too strange. Too much of that
May lead you bye and bye through gloomy lanes
To a sad wilderness, where one may grope
Alone, and always, or until he feels
Ferocious and invisible animals
That wait for men and eat them in the dark.
Why do you sit there on the floor so long,
Smiling at me while I try to be solemn?

Do you not hear it said for your salvation,
When I say truth? Are you, at four and twenty,
So little deceived in us that you interpret
The humor of a woman to be noticed
As her choice between you and Acheron?
Are you so unscathed yet as to infer
That if a woman worries when a man,
Or a man-child, has wet shoes on his feet
She may as well commemorate with ashes
The last eclipse of her tranquillity?
If you look up at me and blink again,
I shall not have to make you tell me lies
To know the letters you have not been reading.
I see now that I may have had for nothing
A most unpleasant shivering in my conscience
When I laid open for your contemplation
The wealth of my worn casket. If I did,
The fault was not yours wholly. Search again
This wreckage we may call for sport a face,
And you may chance upon the price of havoc
That I have paid for a few sorry stones

That shine and have no light—yet once were stars
And sparkled on a crown. Little and weak
They seem; and they are cold, I fear, for you.
But they that once were fire for me may not
Be cold again for me until I die;
And only God knows if they may be then.
There is a love that ceases to be love
In being ourselves. How, then, are we to lose it?
You that are sure that you know everything
There is to know of love, answer me that.
Well? . . . You are not even interested.

Once on a far off time when I was young,
I felt with your assurance, and all through me,
That I had undergone the last and worst
Of love's inventions. There was a boy who brought
The sun with him and woke me up with it,
And that was every morning; every night
I tried to dream of him, but never could,
More than I might have seen in Adam's eyes
Their fond uncertainty when Eve began
The play that all her tireless progeny
Are not yet weary of. One scene of it
Was brief, but was eternal while it lasted;
And that was while I was the happiest
Of an imaginary six or seven,
Somewhere in history but not on earth,
For whom the sky had shaken and let stars
Rain down like diamonds. Then there were clouds,
And a sad end of diamonds; whereupon
Despair came, like a blast that would have brought
Tears to the eyes of all the bears in Finland,
And love was done. That was how much I knew.
Poor little wretch! I wonder where he is
This afternoon. Out of this rain, I hope.

At last, when I had seen so many days
Dressed all alike, and in their marching order,

Go by me that I would not always count them,
One stopped—shattering the whole file of Time,
Or so it seemed; and when I looked again,
There was a man. He struck once with his eyes,
And then there was a woman. I, who had come
To wisdom, or to vision, or what you like,
By the old hidden road that has no name,—
I, who was used to seeing without flying
So much that others fly from without seeing,
Still looked, and was afraid, and looked again.
And after that, when I had read the story
Told in his eyes, and felt within my heart
The bleeding wound of their necessity,
I knew the fear was his. If I had failed him
And flown away from him, I should have lost
Ingloriously my wings in scrambling back,
And found them arms again. If he had struck me
Not only with his eyes but with his hands,
I might have pitied him and hated love,
And then gone mad. I, who have been so strong—
Why don't you laugh?—might even have done all that.
I, who have learned so much, and said so much,
And had the commendations of the great
For one who rules herself—why don't you cry?—
And own a certain small authority
Among the blind, who see no more than ever,
But like my voice,—I would have tossed it all
To Tophet for one man; and he was jealous.
I would have wound a snake around my neck
And then have let it bite me till I died,
If my so doing would have made me sure
That one man might have lived; and he was jealous.
I would have driven these hands into a cage
That held a thousand scorpions, and crushed them,
If only by so poisonous a trial
I could have crushed his doubt. I would have wrung
My living blood with mediaeval engines
Out of my screaming flesh, if only that

182

Would have made one man sure. I would have paid
For him the tiresome price of body and soul,
And let the lash of a tongue-weary town
Fall as it might upon my blistered name;
And while it fell I could have laughed at it,
Knowing that he had found out finally
Where the wrong was. But there was evil in him
That would have made no more of his possession
Than confirmation of another fault;
And there was honor—if you call it honor
That hoods itself with doubt and wears a crown
Of lead that might as well be gold and fire.
Give it as heavy or as light a name
As any there is that fits. I see myself
Without the power to swear to this or that
That I might be if he had been without it.
Whatever I might have been that I was not,
It only happened that it wasn't so.
Meanwhile, you might seem to be listening:
If you forget yourself and go to sleep,
My treasure, I shall not say this again.
Look up once more into my poor old face,
Where you see beauty, or the Lord knows what,
And say to me aloud what else there is
Than ruins in it that you most admire.

No, there was never anything like that;
Nature has never fastened such a mask
Of radiant and impenetrable merit
On any woman as you say there is
On this one. Not a mask? I thank you, sir,
But you see more with your determination,
I fear, than with your prudence or your conscience;
And you have never met me with my eyes
In all the mirrors I've made faces at.
No, I shall never call you strange again:
You are the young and inconvincible
Epitome of all blind men since Adam.

May the blind lead the blind, if that be so?
And we shall need no mirrors? You are saying
What most I feared you might. But if the blind,
Or one of them, be not so fortunate
As to put out the eyes of recollection,
She might at last, without her meaning it,
Lead on the other, without his knowing it,
Until the two of them should lose themselves
Among dead craters in a lava-field
As empty as a desert on the moon.
I am not speaking in a theatre,
But in a room so real and so familiar
That sometimes I would wreck it. Then I pause,
Remembering there is a King in Weimar—
A monarch, and a poet, and a shepherd
Of all who are astray and are outside
The realm where they should rule. I think of him,
And save the furniture; I think of you,
And am forlorn, finding in you the one
To lavish aspirations and illusions
Upon a faded and forsaken house
Where love, being locked alone, was nigh to burning
House and himself together. Yes, you are strange,
To see in such an injured architecture
Room for new love to live in. Are you laughing?
No? Well, you are not crying, as you should be.
Tears, even if they told only gratitude
For your escape, and had no other story,
Were surely more becoming than a smile
For my unwomanly straightforwardness
In seeing for you, through my close gate of years
Your forty ways to freedom. Why do you smile?
And while I'm trembling at my faith in you
In giving you to read this book of danger
That only one man living might have written—
These letters, which have been a part of me
So long that you may read them all again
As often as you look into my face,

And hear them when I speak to you, and feel them
Whenever you have to touch me with your hand,—
Why are you so unwilling to be spared?
Why do you still believe in me? But no,
I'll find another way to ask you that.
I wonder if there is another way
That says it better, and means anything.
There is no other way that could be worse?
I was not asking you; it was myself
Alone that I was asking. Why do I dip
For lies, when there is nothing in my well
But shining truth, you say? How do you know?
Truth has a lonely life down where she lives;
And many a time, when she comes up to breathe,
She sinks before we seize her, and makes ripples.
Possibly you may know no more of me
Than a few ripples; and they may soon be gone,
Leaving you then with all my shining truth
Drowned in a shining water; and when you look
You may not see me there, but something else
That never was a woman—being yourself.
You say to me my truth is past all drowning,
And safe with you for ever? You know all that?
How do you know all that, and who has told you?
You know so much that I'm an atom frightened
Because you know so little. And what is this?
You know the luxury there is in haunting
The blasted thoroughfares of disillusion—
If that's your name for them—with only ghosts
For company? You know that when a woman
Is blessed, or cursed, with a divine impatience
(Another name of yours for a bad temper)
She must have one at hand on whom to wreak it
(That's what you mean, whatever the turn you give it),
Sure of a kindred sympathy, and thereby
Effect a mutual calm? You know that wisdom,
Given in vain to make a food for those
Who are without it, will be seen at last,

And even at last only by those who gave it,
As one or more of the forgotten crumbs
That others leave? You know that men's applause
And women's envy savor so much of dust
That I go hungry, having at home no fare
But the same changeless bread that I may swallow
Only with tears and prayers? Who told you that?
You know that if I read, and read alone,
Too many books that no men yet have written,
I may go blind, or worse? You know yourself,
Of all insistent and insidious creatures,
To be the one to save me, and to guard
For me their flaming language? And you know
That if I give much headway to the whim
That's in me never to be quite sure that even
Through all those years of storm and fire I waited
For this one rainy day, I may go on,
And on, and on alone, through smoke and ashes,
To a cold end? You know so dismal much
As that about me? . . . Well, I believe you do.

LATE SUMMER

(ALCAICS)

CONFUSED, he found her lavishing feminine
Gold upon clay, and found her inscrutable;
    And yet she smiled. Why, then, should horrors
Be as they were, without end, her playthings?

And why were dead years hungrily telling her
Lies of the dead, who told them again to her?
    If now she knew, there might be kindness
Clamoring yet where a faith lay stifled.

A little faith in him, and the ruinous
Past would be for time to annihilate,
    And wash out, like a tide that washes
Out of the sand what a child has drawn there.

God, what a shining handful of happiness,
Made out of days and out of eternities,
    Were now the pulsing end of patience—
Could he but have what a ghost had stolen!

What was a man before him, or ten of them,
While he was here alive who could answer them,
    And in their teeth fling confirmations
Harder than agates against an egg-shell?

But now the man was dead, and would come again
Never, though she might honor ineffably
    The flimsy wraith of him she conjured
Out of a dream with his wand of absence.

And if the truth were now but a mummery,
Meriting pride's implacable irony,
    So much the worse for pride. Moreover,
Save her or fail, there was conscience always.

Meanwhile, a few misgivings of innocence,
Imploring to be sheltered and credited,
    Were not amiss when she revealed them.
Whether she struggled or not, he saw them.

Also, he saw that while she was hearing him
Her eyes had more and more of the past in them;
    And while he told what cautious honor
Told him was all he had best be sure of,

He wondered once or twice, inadvertently,
Where shifting winds were driving his argosies,

Long anchored and as long unladen,
Over the foam for the golden chances.

"If men were not for killing so carelessly,
And women were for wiser endurances,"
    He said, "we might have yet a world here
Fitter for Truth to be seen abroad in;

"If Truth were not so strange in her nakedness,
And we were less forbidden to look at it,
    We might not have to look." He stared then
Down at the sand where the tide threw forward

Its cold, unconquered lines, that unceasingly
Foamed against hope, and fell. He was calm enough,
    Although he knew he might be silenced
Out of all calm; and the night was coming.

"I climb for you the peak of his infamy
That you may choose your fall if you cling to it.
    No more for me unless you say more.
All you have left of a dream defends you:

"The truth may be as evil an augury
As it was needful now for the two of us.
    We cannot have the dead between us.
Tell me to go, and I go."—She pondered:

"What you believe is right for the two of us
Makes it as right that you are not one of us.
    If this be needful truth you tell me,
Spare me, and let me have lies hereafter."

She gazed away where shadows were covering
The whole cold ocean's healing indifference.
    No ship was coming. When the darkness
Fell, she was there, and alone, still gazing.

AN EVANGELIST'S WIFE

"WHY am I not myself these many days,
You ask? And have you nothing more to ask?
I do you wrong? I do not hear your praise
To God for giving you me to share your task?

"Jealous—of Her? Because her cheeks are pink,
And she has eyes? No, not if she had seven.
If you should only steal an hour to think,
Sometime, there might be less to be forgiven.

"No, you are never cruel. If once or twice
I found you so, I could applaud and sing.
Jealous of—What? You are not very wise.
Does not the good Book tell you anything?

"In David's time poor Michal had to go.
Jealous of God? Well, if you like it so."

From

AVON'S

HARVEST,

ETC.

1921

———•◦•———

To

Seth Ellis

Pope

MR. FLOOD'S PARTY

OLD Eben Flood, climbing alone one night
Over the hill between the town below
And the forsaken upland hermitage
That held as much as he should ever know
On earth again of home, paused warily.
The road was his with not a native near;
And Eben, having leisure, said aloud,
For no man else in Tilbury Town to hear:

"Well, Mr. Flood, we have the harvest moon
Again, and we may not have many more;
The bird is on the wing, the poet says,
And you and I have said it here before.
Drink to the bird." He raised up to the light
The jug that he had gone so far to fill,
And answered huskily: "Well, Mr. Flood,
Since you propose it, I believe I will."

Alone, as if enduring to the end
A valiant armor of scarred hopes outworn,
He stood there in the middle of the road
Like Roland's ghost winding a silent horn.
Below him, in the town among the trees,
Where friends of other days had honored him,
A phantom salutation of the dead
Rang thinly till old Eben's eyes were dim.

Then, as a mother lays her sleeping child
Down tenderly, fearing it may awake,
He set the jug down slowly at his feet
With trembling care, knowing that most things break;
And only when assured that on firm earth
It stood, as the uncertain lives of men
Assuredly did not, he paced away,
And with his hand extended paused again:

"Well, Mr. Flood, we have not met like this
In a long time; and many a change has come
To both of us, I fear, since last it was
We had a drop together. Welcome home!"
Convivially returning with himself,
Again he raised the jug up to the light;
And with an acquiescent quaver said:
"Well, Mr. Flood, if you insist, I might.

"Only a very little, Mr. Flood—
For auld lang syne. No more, sir; that will do."
So, for the time, apparently it did,
And Eben evidently thought so too;
For soon amid the silver loneliness
Of night he lifted up his voice and sang,
Secure, with only two moons listening,
Until the whole harmonious landscape rang—

"For auld lang syne." The weary throat gave out;
The last word wavered, and the song was done.
He raised again the jug regretfully
And shook his head, and was again alone.
There was not much that was ahead of him,
And there was nothing in the town below—
Where strangers would have shut the many doors
That many friends had opened long ago.

BEN TROVATO

The deacon thought. "I know them," he began,
"And they are all you ever heard of them—
Allurable to no sure theorem,
The scorn or the humility of man.

194

You say 'Can I believe it?'—and I can;
And I'm unwilling even to condemn
The benefaction of a stratagem
Like hers—and I'm a Presbyterian.

"Though blind, with but a wandering hour to live,
He felt the other woman in the fur
That now the wife had on. Could she forgive
All that? Apparently. Her rings were gone,
Of course; and when he found that she had none,
He smiled—as he had never smiled at her."

THE TREE IN PAMELA'S GARDEN

PAMELA was too gentle to deceive
Her roses. "Let the men stay where they are,"
She said, "and if Apollo's avatar
Be one of them, I shall not have to grieve."
And so she made all Tilbury Town believe
She sighed a little more for the North Star
Than over men, and only in so far
As she was in a garden was like Eve.

Her neighbors—doing all that neighbors can
To make romance of reticence meanwhile—
Seeing that she had never loved a man,
Wished Pamela had a cat, or a small bird,
And only would have wondered at her smile
Could they have seen that she had overheard.

VAIN GRATUITIES

Never was there a man much uglier
In eyes of other women, or more grim:
"The Lord has filled her chalice to the brim,
So let us pray she's a philosopher,"
They said; and there was more they said of her—
Deeming it, after twenty years with him,
No wonder that she kept her figure slim
And always made you think of lavender.

But she, demure as ever, and as fair,
Almost, as they remembered her before
She found him, would have laughed had she been there;
And all they said would have been heard no more
Than foam that washes on an island shore
Where there are none to listen or to care.

LOST ANCHORS

Like a dry fish flung inland far from shore,
There lived a sailor, warped and ocean-browned,
Who told of an old vessel, harbor-drowned
And out of mind a century before,
Where divers, on descending to explore
A legend that had lived its way around
The world of ships, in the dark hulk had found
Anchors, which had been seized and seen no more.

Improving a dry leisure to invest
Their misadventure with a manifest
Analogy that he may read who runs,
The sailor made it old as ocean grass—
Telling of much that once had come to pass
With him, whose mother should have had no sons.

MONADNOCK THROUGH THE TREES

BEFORE there was in Egypt any sound
Of those who reared a more prodigious means
For the self-heavy sleep of kings and queens
Than hitherto had mocked the most renowned,—
Unvisioned here and waiting to be found,
Alone, amid remote and older scenes,
You loomed above ancestral evergreens
Before there were the first of us around.

And when the last of us, if we know how,
See farther from ourselves than we do now,
Assured with other sight than heretofore
That we have done our mortal best and worst,—
Your calm will be the same as when the first
Assyrians went howling south to war.

MANY ARE CALLED

THE Lord Apollo, who has never died,
Still holds alone his immemorial reign,
Supreme in an impregnable domain
That with his magic he has fortified;
And though melodious multitudes have tried
In ecstasy, in anguish, and in vain,
With invocation sacred and profane
To lure him, even the loudest are outside.

Only at unconjectured intervals,
By will of him on whom no man may gaze,
By word of him whose law no man has read,
A questing light may rift the sullen walls,
To cling where mostly its infrequent rays
Fall golden on the patience of the dead.

REMBRANDT TO REMBRANDT

(AMSTERDAM, 1645)

AND there you are again, now as you are.
Observe yourself as you discern yourself
In your discredited ascendency;
Without your velvet or your feathers now,
Commend your new condition to your fate,
And your conviction to the sieves of time.
Meanwhile appraise yourself, Rembrandt van Ryn,
Now as you are—formerly more or less
Distinguished in the civil scenery,
And once a painter. There you are again,
Where you may see that you have on your shoulders
No lovelier burden for an ornament
Than one man's head that's yours. Praise be to God
That you have that; for you are like enough
To need it now, my friend, and from now on;
For there are shadows and obscurities
Immediate or impending on your view,
That may be worse than you have ever painted
For the bewildered and unhappy scorn
Of injured Hollanders in Amsterdam
Who cannot find their fifty florins' worth
Of Holland face where you have hidden it
In your new golden shadow that excites them,
Or see that when the Lord made color and light
He made not one thing only, or believe
That shadows are not nothing. Saskia said,
Before she died, how they would swear at you,
And in commiseration at themselves.
She laughed a little, too, to think of them—
And then at me. . . . That was before she died.

And I could wonder, as I look at you,
There as I have you now, there as you are,
Or nearly so as any skill of mine
Has ever caught you in a bilious mirror,—

Yes, I could wonder long, and with a reason,
If all but everything achievable
In me were not achieved and lost already,
Like a fool's gold. But you there in the glass,
And you there on the canvas, have a sort
Of solemn doubt about it; and that's well
For Rembrandt and for Titus. All that's left
Of all that was is here; and all that's here
Is one man who remembers, and one child
Beginning to forget. One, two, and three,
The others died, and then—then Saskia died;
And then, so men believe, the painter died.
So men believe. So it all comes at once.
And here's a fellow painting in the dark,—
A loon who cannot see that he is dead
Before God lets him die. He paints away
At the impossible, so Holland has it,
For venom or for spite, or for defection,
Or else for God knows what. Well, if God knows,
And Rembrandt knows, it matters not so much
What Holland knows or cares. If Holland wants
Its heads all in a row, and all alike,
There's Franz to do them and to do them well—
Rat-catchers, archers, or apothecaries,
And one as like a rabbit as another.
Value received, and every Dutchman happy.
All's one to Franz, and to the rest of them,—
Their ways being theirs, are theirs.—But you, my friend,
If I have made you something as you are,
Will need those jaws and eyes and all the fight
And fire that's in them, and a little more,
To take you on and the world after you;
For now you fare alone, without the fashion
To sing you back and fling a flower or two
At your accusing feet. Poor Saskia saw
This coming that has come, and with a guile
Of kindliness that covered half her doubts
Would give me gold, and laugh . . . before she died.

And if I see the road that you are going,
You that are not so jaunty as aforetime,
God knows if she were not appointed well
To die. She might have wearied of it all
Before the worst was over, or begun.
A woman waiting on a man's avouch
Of the invisible, may not wait always
Without a word betweenwhiles, or a dash
Of poison on his faith. Yes, even she,
She might have come to see at last with others,
And then to say with others, who say more,
That you are groping on a phantom trail
Determining a dusky way to nowhere;
That errors unconfessed and obstinate
Have teemed and cankered in you for so long
That even your eyes are sick, and you see light
Only because you dare not see the dark
That is around you and ahead of you.
She might have come, by ruinous estimation
Of old applause and outworn vanities,
To clothe you over in a shroud of dreams,
And so be nearer to the counterfeit
Of her invention than aware of yours.
She might, as well as any, by this time,
Unwillingly and eagerly have bitten
Another devil's-apple of unrest,
And so, by some attendant artifice
Or other, might anon have had you sharing
A taste that would have tainted everything,
And so had been for two, instead of one,
The taste of death in life—which is the food
Of art that has betrayed itself alive
And is a food of hell. She might have heard
Unhappily the temporary noise
Of louder names than yours, and on frail urns
That hardly will ensure a dwelling-place
For even the dust that may be left of them,
She might, and angrily, as like as not,

Look soon to find your name, not finding it.
She might, like many another born for joy
And for sufficient fulness of the hour,
Go famishing by now, and in the eyes
Of pitying friends and dwindling satellites
Be told of no uncertain dereliction
Touching the cold offence of my decline.
And even if this were so, and she were here
Again to make a fact of all my fancy,
How should I ask of her to see with me
Through night where many a time I seem in vain
To seek for new assurance of a gleam
That comes at last, and then, so it appears,
Only for you and me—and a few more,
Perchance, albeit their faces are not many
Among the ruins that are now around us.
That was a fall, my friend, we had together—
Or rather it was my house, mine alone,
That fell, leaving you safe. Be glad for that.
There's life in you that shall outlive my clay
That's for a time alive and will in time
Be nothing—but not yet. You that are there
Where I have painted you are safe enough,
Though I see dragons. Verily, that was a fall—
A dislocating fall, a blinding fall,
A fall indeed. But there are no bones broken;
And even the teeth and eyes that I make out
Among the shadows, intermittently,
Show not so firm in their accoutrement
Of terror-laden unreality
As you in your neglect of their performance,—
Though for their season we must humor them
For what they are: devils undoubtedly,
But not so perilous and implacable
In their undoing of poor human triumph
As easy fashion—or brief novelty
That ails even while it grows, and like sick fruit
Falls down anon to an indifferent earth

To break with inward rot. I say all this,
And I concede, in honor of your silence,
A waste of innocent facility
In tints of other colors than are mine.
I cannot paint with words, but there's a time
For most of us when words are all we have
To serve our stricken souls. And here you say,
"Be careful, or you may commit your soul
Soon to the very devil of your denial."
I might have wagered on you to say that,
Knowing that I believe in you too surely
To spoil you with a kick or paint you over.

No, my good friend, Mynheer Rembrandt van Ryn—
Sometime a personage in Amsterdam,
But now not much—I shall not give myself
To be the sport of any dragon-spawn
Of Holland, or elsewhere. Holland was hell
Not long ago, and there were dragons then
More to be fought than any of these we see
That we may foster now. They are not real,
But not for that the less to be regarded;
For there are slimy tyrants born of nothing
That harden slowly into seeming life
And have the strength of madness. I confess,
Accordingly, the wisdom of your care
That I look out for them. Whether I would
Or not, I must; and here we are as one
With our necessity. For though you loom
A little harsh in your respect of time
And circumstance, and of ordained eclipse,
We know together of a golden flood
That with its overflow shall drown away
The dikes that held it; and we know thereby
That in its rising light there lives a fire
No devils that are lodging here in Holland
Shall put out wholly, or much agitate,
Except in unofficial preparation

They put out first the sun. It's well enough
To think of them; wherefore I thank you, sir,
Alike for your remembrance and attention.

But there are demons that are longer-lived
Than doubts that have a brief and evil term
To congregate among the futile shards
And architraves of eminent collapse.
They are a many-favored family,
All told, with not a misbegotten dwarf
Among the rest that I can love so little
As one occult abortion in especial
Who perches on a picture (when it's done)
And says, "What of it, Rembrandt, if you do?"
This incubus would seem to be a sort
Of chorus, indicating, for our good,
The silence of the few friends that are left:
"What of it, Rembrandt, even if you know?"
It says again; "and you don't know for certain.
What if in fifty or a hundred years
They find you out? You may have gone meanwhile
So greatly to the dogs that you'll not care
Much what they find. If this be all you are—
This unaccountable aspiring insect—
You'll sleep as easy in oblivion
As any sacred monk or parricide;
And if, as you conceive, you are eternal,
Your soul may laugh, remembering (if a soul
Remembers) your befrenzied aspiration
To smear with certain ochres and some oil
A few more perishable ells of cloth,
And once or twice, to square your vanity,
Prove it was you alone that should achieve
A mortal eye—that may, no less, tomorrow
Show an immortal reason why today
Men see no more. And what's a mortal eye
More than a mortal herring, who has eyes
As well as you? Why not paint herrings, Rembrandt?

Or if not herrings, why not a split beef?
Perceive it only in its unalloyed
Integrity, and you may find in it
A beautified accomplishment no less
Indigenous than one that appertains
To gentlemen and ladies eating it.
The same God planned and made you, beef and human;
And one, but for His whim, might be the other."

That's how he says it, Rembrandt, if you listen;
He says it, and he goes. And then, sometimes,
There comes another spirit in his place—
One with a more engaging argument,
And with a softer note for saying truth
Not soft. Whether it be the truth or not,
I name it so; for there's a string in me
Somewhere that answers—which is natural,
Since I am but a living instrument
Played on by powers that are invisible.
"You might go faster, if not quite so far,"
He says, "if in your vexed economy
There lived a faculty for saying yes
And meaning no, and then for doing neither;
But since Apollo sees it otherwise,
Your Dutchmen, who are swearing at you still
For your pernicious filching of their florins,
May likely curse you down their generation,
Not having understood there was no malice
Or grinning evil in a golden shadow
That shall outshine their slight identities
And hold their faces when their names are nothing.
But this, as you discern, or should by now
Surmise, for you is neither here nor there:
You made your picture as your demon willed it;
That's about all of that. Now make as many
As may be to be made,—for so you will,
Whatever the toll may be, and hold your light
So that you see, without so much to blind you

As even the cobweb-flash of a misgiving,
Assured and certain that if you see right
Others will have to see—albeit their seeing
Shall irk them out of their serenity
For such a time as umbrage may require.
But there are many reptiles in the night
That now is coming on, and they are hungry;
And there's a Rembrandt to be satisfied
Who never will be, howsoever much
He be assured of an ascendency
That has not yet a shadow's worth of sound
Where Holland has its ears. And what of that?
Have you the weary leisure or sick wit
That breeds of its indifference a false envy
That is the vermin on accomplishment?
Are you inaugurating your new service
With fasting for a food you would not eat?
You are the servant, Rembrandt, not the master,—
But you are not assigned with other slaves
That in their freedom are the most in fear.
One of the few that are so fortunate
As to be told their task and to be given
A skill to do it with a tool too keen
For timid safety, bow your elected head
Under the stars tonight, and whip your devils
Each to his nest in hell. Forget your days,
And so forgive the years that may not be
So many as to be more than you may need
For your particular consistency
In your peculiar folly. You are counting
Some fewer years than forty at your heels;
And they have not pursued your gait so fast
As your oblivion—which has beaten them,
And rides now on your neck like an old man
With iron shins and fingers. Let him ride
(You haven't so much to say now about that),
And in a proper season let him run.
You may be dead then, even as you may now

Anticipate some other mortal strokes
Attending your felicity; and for that,
Oblivion heretofore has done some running
Away from graves, and will do more of it."

That's how it is your wiser spirit speaks,
Rembrandt. If you believe him, why complain?
If not, why paint? And why, in any event,
Look back for the old joy and the old roses,
Or the old fame? They are all gone together,
And Saskia with them; and with her left out,
They would avail no more now than one strand
Of Samson's hair wound round his little finger
Before the temple fell. Nor more are you
In any sudden danger to forget
That in Apollo's house there are no clocks
Or calendars to say for you in time
How far you are away from Amsterdam,
Or that the one same law that bids you see
Where now you see alone forbids in turn
Your light from Holland eyes till Holland ears
Are told of it; for that way, my good fellow,
Is one way more to death. If at the first
Of your long turning, which may still be longer
Than even your faith has measured it, you sigh
For distant welcome that may not be seen,
Or wayside shouting that will not be heard,
You may as well accommodate your greatness
To the convenience of an easy ditch,
And, anchored there with all your widowed gold,
Forget your darkness in the dark, and hear
No longer the cold wash of Holland scorn.

From

DIONYSUS

IN DOUBT

1925

———•••———

To

Craven Langstroth

Betts

HAUNTED HOUSE

HERE was a place where none would ever come
For shelter, save as we did from the rain.
We saw no ghost, yet once outside again
Each wondered why the other should be dumb;
For we had fronted nothing worse than gloom
And ruin, and to our vision it was plain
Where thrift, outshivering fear, had let remain
Some chairs that were like skeletons of home.

There were no trackless footsteps on the floor
Above us, and there were no sounds elsewhere.
But there was more than sound; and there was more
Than just an axe that once was in the air
Between us and the chimney, long before
Our time. So townsmen said who found her there.

THE SHEAVES

WHERE long the shadows of the wind had rolled,
Green wheat was yielding to the change assigned;
And as by some vast magic undivined
The world was turning slowly into gold.
Like nothing that was ever bought or sold
It waited there, the body and the mind;
And with a mighty meaning of a kind
That tells the more the more it is not told.

So in a land where all days are not fair,
Fair days went on till on another day
A thousand golden sheaves were lying there,
Shining and still, but not for long to stay—
As if a thousand girls with golden hair
Might rise from where they slept and go away.

209

KARMA

CHRISTMAS was in the air and all was well
With him, but for a few confusing flaws
In divers of God's images. Because
A friend of his would neither buy nor sell,
Was he to answer for the axe that fell?
He pondered; and the reason for it was,
Partly, a slowly freezing Santa Claus
Upon the corner, with his beard and bell.

Acknowledging an improvident surprise,
He magnified a fancy that he wished
The friend whom he had wrecked were here again.
Not sure of that, he found a compromise;
And from the fulness of his heart he fished
A dime for Jesus who had died for men.

A MAN IN OUR TOWN

WE pitied him as one too much at ease
With Nemesis and impending indigence;
Also, as if by way of recompense,
We sought him always in extremities;
And while ways more like ours had more to please
Our common code than his improvidence,
There lurked alive in our experience
His homely genius for emergencies.

He was not one for men to marvel at,
And yet there was another neighborhood
When he was gone, and many a thrifty tear.
There was an increase in a man like that;
And though he be forgotten, it was good
For more than one of you that he was here.

EN PASSANT

I should have glanced and passed him, naturally,
But his designs and mine were opposite;
He spoke, and having temporized a bit,
He said that he was going to the sea:
"I've watched on highways for so long," said he,
"That I'll go down there to be sure of it."
And all at once his famished eyes were lit
With a wrong light—or so it was to me.

That evening there was talk along the shore
Of one who shot a stranger, saying first:
"You should have come when called. This afternoon
A gentleman unknown to me before,
With deference always due to souls accurst,
Came out of his own grave—and not too soon."

GLASS HOUSES

Learn if you must, but do not come to me
For truth of what your pleasant neighbor says
Behind you of your looks or of your ways,
Or of your worth and virtue generally;
If he's a pleasure to you, let him be—
Being the same to him; and let your days
Be tranquil, having each the other's praise,
And each his own opinion peaceably.

Two others once did love each other well,
Yet not so well but that a pungent word
From each came stinging home to the wrong ears.
The rest would be an overflow to tell,
Surely; and you may slowly have inferred
That you may not be here a thousand years.

MORTMAIN

Avenel Gray at fifty had gray hair,
Gray eyes, and a gray cat—coincidence
Agreeable enough to be approved
And shared by all her neighbors; or by all
Save one, who had, in his abused esteem,
No share of it worth having. Avenel Gray
At fifty had the favor and the grace
Of thirty—the gray hair being only a jest
Of time, he reasoned, whereby the gray eyes
Were maybe twenty or maybe a thousand.
Never could he persuade himself to say
How old or young they were, or what was in them,
Or whether in the mind or in the heart
Of their possessor there had ever been,
Or ever should be, more than room enough
For the undying dead. All he could say
Would be that she was now to him a child,
A little frightened or a little vexed,
And now a sort of Miss Methuselah,
Adept and various in obscurity
And in omniscience rather terrible—
Until she smiled and was a child again,
Seeing with eyes that had no age in them
That his were growing older. Seneca Sprague
At fifty had hair grayer, such as it was,
Than Avenel's—an atoll, as it were,
Circling a smooth lagoon of indignation,
Whereunder were concealed no treacheries
Or monsters that were perilous to provoke.

Seneca sat one Sunday afternoon
With Avenel in her garden. There was peace
And languor in the air, but in his mind
There was not either—there was Avenel;
And where she was, and she was everywhere,
There was no peace for Seneca. So today

Should see the last of him in any garden
Where a sphynx-child, with gray eyes and gray hair,
Would be the only flower that he might wish
To pluck, wishing in vain. "I'm here again,"
Seneca said, "and I'm not here alone;
You may observe that I've a guest with me
This time, Time being the guest—scythe, glass, and all.
Time is a guest not given to a long waiting,
And, in so far as you may not have known it,
I'm Destiny. For more than twenty years
My search has been for an identity
Worth Time's acknowledgment; and heretofore
My search has been but a long faltering,
Paid with an unavailing gratitude
And unconfessed encouragement from you.
What is it in me that you like so much,
And love so little? I'm not so much a monkey
As many who have had their heart's desire,
And have it still. My perishable angel,
Since neither you nor I may live forever
Like this, I'll say the folly that has fooled us
Out of our lives was never mine, but yours.
There was an understanding long ago
Between the laws and atoms that your life
And mine together were to be a triumph;
But one contingency was overlooked,
And that was a complete one. All you love,
And all you dare to love, is far from here—
Too far for me to find where I am going."
"Going?" Avenel said. "Where are you going?"
There was a frightened wonder in her eyes,
Until she found a way for them to laugh:
"At first I thought you might be going to tell me
That you had found a new way to be old—
Maybe without remembering all the time
How gray we are. But when you soon began
To be so unfamiliar and ferocious—
Well, I began to wonder. I'm a woman."

Seneca sighed before he shook his head
At Avenel: "You say you are a woman,
And I suppose you are. If you are not,
I don't know what you are; and if you are,
I don't know what you mean."

                                    "By what?" she said.
A faint bewildered flush covered her face,
While Seneca felt within her voice a note
As near to sharpness as a voice like hers
Might have in silent hiding. "What have I done
So terrible all at once that I'm a stranger?"

"You are no stranger than you always were,"
He said, "and you are not required to be so.
You are no stranger now than yesterday,
Or twenty years ago; or thirty years
Longer ago than that, when you were born—
You and your brother. I'm not here to scare you,
Or to pour any measure of reproach
Out of a surplus urn of chilly wisdom;
For watching you to find out whether or not
You shivered swallowing it would be no joy
For me. But since it has all come to this—
Which is the same as nothing, only worse,
I am not either wise or kind enough,
It seems, to go away from you in silence.
My wonder is today that I have been
So long in finding what there was to find,
Or rather in recognizing what I found
Long since and hid with incredulities
That years have worn away, leaving white bones
Before me in a desert. All those bones,
If strung together, would be a skeleton
That once upheld a living form of hope
For me to follow until at last it fell
Where there was only sand and emptiness.
For a long time there was not even a grave—

Hope having died there all alone, you see,
And in the dark. And you, being as you are,
Inseparable from your obsession—well,
I went so far last evening as to fancy,
Having no other counsellor than myself
To guide me, that you might be entertained,
If not instructed, hearing how far I wandered,
Following hope into an empty desert,
And what I found there. If we never know
What we have found, and are accordingly
Adrift upon the wreck of our invention,
We make our way as quietly to shore
As possible, and we say no more about it;
But if we know too well for our well-being
That what it is we know had best be shared
With one who knows too much of it already,
Even kindliness becomes, or may become,
A strangling and unwilling incubus.
A ghost would often help us if he could,
But being a ghost he can't. I may confuse
Regret with wisdom, but in going so far
As not impossibly to be annoying,
My wish is that you see the part you are
Of nature. When you find anomalies here
Among your flowers and are surprised at them,
Consider yourself and be surprised again;
For they and their potential oddities
Are all a part of nature. So are you,
Though you be not a part that nature favors,
And favoring, carries on. You are a monster;
A most adorable and essential monster."

He watched her face and waited, but she gave him
Only a baffled glance before there fell
So great a silence there among the flowers
That even their fragrance had almost a sound;
And some that had no fragrance may have had,
He fancied, an accusing voice of color

Which her pale cheeks now answered with another;
Wherefore he gazed a while at tiger-lilies
Hollyhocks, dahlias, asters and hydrangeas—
The generals of an old anonymous host
That he knew only by their shapes and faces.
Beyond them he saw trees; and beyond them
A still blue summer sky where there were stars
In hiding, as there might somewhere be veiled
Eternal reasons why the tricks of time
Were played like this. Two insects on a leaf
Would fill about as much of nature's eye,
No doubt, as would a woman and a man
At odds with heritage. Yet there they sat,
A woman and a man, beyond the range
Of all deceit and all philosophy
To make them less or larger than they were.
The sun might only be a spark among
Superior stars, but one could not help that.

"If a grim God that watches each of us
In turn, like an old-fashioned schoolmaster,"
Seneca said, still gazing at the blue
Beyond the trees, "no longer satisfies,
Or tortures our credulity with harps
Or fires, who knows if there may not be laws
Harder for us to vanquish or evade
Than any tyrants? Rather, we know there are;
Or you would not be studying butterflies
While I'm encouraging Empedocles
In retrospect. He was a mountain-climber,
You may remember; and while I think of him,
I think if only there were more volcanoes,
More of us might be climbing to their craters
To find out what he found. You are sufficient,
You and your cumulative silences
Today, to make of his abysmal ashes
The dust of all our logic and our faith;
And since you can do that, you must have power

That you have never measured. Or, if you like,
A power too large for any measurement
Has done it for you, made you as you are,
And led me for the last time, possibly,
To bow before a phantom in your garden."
He smiled—until he saw tears in her eyes,
And then remarked, "Here comes a friend of yours.
Pyrrhus, you call him. Pyrrhus because he purrs."

"I found him reading Hamlet," Avenel said;
"By which I mean that I was reading Hamlet.
But he's an old cat now. And I'm another—
If you mean what you say, or seem to say.
If not, what in the world's name do you mean?"

He met the futile question with a question
Almost as futile and almost as old:
"Why have I been so long learning to read,
Or learning to be willing to believe
That I was learning? All that I had to do
Was to remember that your brother once
Was here, and is here still. Why have I waited—
Why have you made me wait—so long to say so?"
Although he said it kindly, and foresaw
That in his kindness would be pain, he said it—
More to the blue beyond the trees, perhaps,
Or to the stars that moved invisibly
To laws implacable and inviolable,
Than to the stricken ears of Avenel,
Who looked at him as if to speak. He waited,
Until it seemed that all the leaves and flowers,
The butterflies and the cat, were waiting also.

"Am I the only woman alive," she asked,
"Who has a brother she may not forget?
If you are here to be mysterious,
Ingenuousness like mine may disappoint you.
And there are women somewhere, certainly,

Riper for mysteries than I am yet.
You see me living always in one place,
And all alone."

               "No, you are not alone,"
Seneca said: "I wish to God you were!
And I wish more that you had been so always,
That you might be so now. Your brother is here,
And yet he has not been here for ten years.
Though you've a skill to crowd your paradigms
Into a cage like that, and keep them there,
You may not yet be asking quite so much
Of others, for whom the present is not the past.
We are not all magicians; and Time himself
Who is already beckoning me away,
Would surely have been cut with his own scythe,
And long ago, if he had followed you
In all your caprioles and divagations.
You have deceived the present so demurely
That only few have been aware of it,
And you the least of all. You do not know
How much it was of you that was not you
That made me wait. And why I was so long
In seeing that it was never to be you,
Is not for you to tell me—for I know.
I was so long in seeing it was not you,
Because I would not see. I wonder, now,
If I should take you up and carry you off,
Like an addressable orang-outang,
You might forget the grave where half of you
Is buried alive, and where the rest of you,
Whatever you may believe it may be doing,
Is perilously employed." As if to save
His mistress the convention of an answer,
The cat jumped up into her lap and purred,
Folded his paws, and looked at Seneca
Suspiciously. "I might almost have done it,"
He said, "if insight and experience

Had not assured me it would do no good.
Don't be afraid. I have tried everything,
Only to be assured it was not you
That made me fail. If you were here alone,
You would not see the last of me so soon;
And even with you and the invisible
Together, maybe I might have seized you then
Just hard enough to leave you black and blue—
Not that you would have cared one way or other,
With him forever near you, and if unseen,
Always a refuge. No, I should not have hurt you.
It would have done no good—yet might perhaps
Have made me likelier to be going away
At the right time. Anyhow, damn the cat."

Seneca looked at Avenel till she smiled,
And so let loose a tear that she had held
In each of her gray eyes. "I am too old,"
She said, "and too incorrigibly alone,
For you to laugh at me. You have been saying
More nonsense in an hour than I have heard
Before in forty years. Why do you do it?
Why do you talk like this of going away?
Where would you be, and what would you be doing?
You would be like a cat in a strange house—
Like Pyrrhus here in yours. I have not had
My years for nothing; and you are not so young
As to be quite so sure that I'm a child.
We are too old to be ridiculous,
And we've been friends too long."

                          "We have been friends
Too long," he said, "to be friends any longer.
And there you have the burden of a song
That I came here to sing this afternoon.
When I said friends you might have halted me,
For I meant neighbors."

                                    "I know what you meant,"
Avenel answered, gazing at the sky,
And then at Seneca. "The great question is,
What made you say it? You mention powers and laws,
As if you understood them. Am I stranger
Than powers and laws that make me as I am?"

"God knows you are no stranger than you are,
For which I praise Him," Seneca said, devoutly.
"I see no need of prayer to bring to pass
For me more prodigies or more difficulties.
I cry for them no longer when I know
That you are married to your brother's ghost,
Even as you were married to your brother—
Never contending or suspecting it,
Yet married all the same. You are alone,
But only in so far as to my eyes
The sight of your beloved is unseen.
Why should I come between you and your ghost,
Whose hand is always chilly on my shoulder,
Drawing me back whenever I go forward?
I should have been acclaimed stronger than he
Before he died, but he can twist me now,
And I resign my dream to his dominion.
And if by chance of an uncertain urge
Of weariness or pity you might essay
The stranglings of a twofold loyalty,
The depth and length and width of my estate,
Measured magnanimously, would be but that
Of half a grave. I'd best be rational,
I'm saying therefore to myself today,
And leave you quiet. I can originate
No reason larger than a leucocyte
Why you should not, since there are two of you,
Be tranquil here together till the end."

"You would not tell me this if it were true,
And I, if it were true, should not believe it,"

Said Avenel, stroking slowly with cold hands
The cat's warm coat. "But I might still be vexed—
Yes, even with you; and that would be a pity.
It may be well for you to go away—
Or for a while—perhaps. I have not heard
Such an unpleasant nonsense anywhere
As this of yours. I like you, Seneca,
But not when you bring Time and Destiny,
As now you do, for company. When you come
Some other day, leave your two friends outside.
We have gone well without them for so long
That we shall hardly be tragedians now,
Not even if we may try; and we have been
Too long familiar with our differences
To quarrel—or to change."

              Avenel smiled
At Seneca with gray eyes wherein were drowned
Inquisitive injuries, and the gray cat yawned
At him as he departed with a sigh
That answered nothing. He went slowly home,
Imagining, as a fond improvisation,
That waves huger than Andes or Sierras
Would soon be overwhelming, as before,
A ship that would be sunk for the last time
With all on board, and far from Tilbury Town.

NEW ENGLAND

HERE where the wind is always north-north-east
And children learn to walk on frozen toes,
Wonder begets an envy of all those
Who boil elsewhere with such a lyric yeast

Of love that you will hear them at a feast
Where demons would appeal for some repose,
Still clamoring where the chalice overflows
And crying wildest who have drunk the least.

Passion is here a soilure of the wits,
We're told, and Love a cross for them to bear;
Joy shivers in the corner where she knits
And Conscience always has the rocking-chair,
Cheerful as when she tortured into fits
The first cat that was ever killed by Care.

BATTLE AFTER WAR

Out of a darkness, into a slow light
That was at first no light that had a name,
Like one thrust up from Erebus he came,
Groping alone, blind with remembered sight.
But there were not those faces in the night,
And all those eyes no longer were aflame
That once he feared and hated, being the same
As his that were the fuel of his fright.

He shone, for one so long among the lost,
Like a stout Roman after Pentecost:
"Terror will yield as much as we dare face
Ourselves in it, and it will yield no more,"
He said. And we see two now in his place,
Where there was room for only one before.

THE GARDEN OF THE NATIONS
(1923)

WHEN we that are the bitten flower and fruit
Of time's achievement are undone between
The blight above, where blight has always been,
And the old worm of evil at the root,
We shall not have to crumble destitute
Of recompense, or measure our chagrin;
We shall be dead, and so shall not be seen
Amid the salvage of our disrepute.

And when we are all gone, shall mightier seeds
And scions of a warmer spring put forth
A bloom and fruitage of a larger worth
Than ours? God save the garden, if by chance,
Or by approved short sight, more numerous weeds
And weevils be the next inheritance!

A CHRISTMAS SONNET
For One in Doubt

WHILE you that in your sorrow disavow
Service and hope, see love and brotherhood
Far off as ever, it will do no good
For you to wear his thorns upon your brow
For doubt of him. And should you question how
To serve him best, he might say, if he could,
"Whether or not the cross was made of wood
Whereon you nailed me, is no matter now."

Though other saviors have in older lore
A Legend, and for older gods have died—
Though death may wear the crown it always wore
And ignorance be still the sword of pride—
Something is here that was not here before,
And strangely has not yet been crucified.

223

From

NICODEMUS

1932

———◆◆———

To

Edwin Carty

Ranck

TOUSSAINT L'OUVERTURE

(CHATEAU DE JOUX, 1803)

AM I alone—or is it you, my friend?
I call you friend, but let it not be known
That such a word was uttered in this place.
You are the first that has forgotten duty
So far as to be sorry—and perilously,
For you—that I am not so frozen yet,
Or starved, or blasted, that I cannot feel.
Yes, I can feel, and hear. I can hear something
Behind me. Is it you? There is no light,
But there's a gray place where a window was
Before the sun went down. Was there a sun?
There must have been one; for there was a light,
Or sort of light—enough to make me see
That I was here alone. Was I forgotten?
I have been here alone now for three days,
Without you, and with nothing here to eat
Or drink; and for God knows how many months,
Or years, before you came, have I been here—
But never alone so long. You must be careful,
Or they will kill you if they hear you asking
Questions of me as if I were a man.
I did not know that there was anything left
Alive to see me, or to consider me,
As more than a transplanted shovelful
Of black earth, with a seed of danger in it—
A seed that's not there now, and never was.
When was I dangerous to Napoleon?
Does a perfidious victor fear the victim
That he has trapped and harassed? No, he hates him.
The only danger that was ever in me
Was food that his hate made to feed itself.
There lives in hate a seed more dangerous
To man, I fear, than any in time's garden
That has not risen to full stalk and flower

In history yet. I am glad now for being
So like a child as to believe in him
As long as there was hope. And what was hope?
Hope was a pebble I brought here to play with,
And might as well have dropped into the ocean
Before there was a bitter league of it
Between me and my island. It was well
Not to do that. Not that it matters now.

My friend, I do not hear you any longer.
Are you still there? Are you afraid to speak?
You are the first thing fashioned as a man
That has acknowledged me since I came here—
To die, as I see now—with word or motion
Of one man in the same world with another;
And you may be afraid of saying to me
Some word that hurts your tongue. Have they invented
A last new misery fit for the last days
Of an old sick black man who says tonight
He does not think that he shall have to live
Much longer now? If there were left in me
A way to laugh, I might as well be laughing
To think of that. Say to Napoleon
That he has made an end of me so slowly,
And thoroughly, that only God Almighty
Shall say what is to say. And if God made him,
And made him as he is, and has to be,
Say who shall answer for a world where men
Are mostly blind, and they who are the blindest
Climb to cold heights that others cannot reach,
And there, with all there is for them to see,
See nothing but themselves. I am not one
To tell you about that, for I am only
A man destroyed, a sick man, soon to die;
A man betrayed, who sees his end a ruin,
Yet cannot see that he has lived in vain.
Though he was crushed and humbled at the last
As things are that are crawling in man's way,

He was a man. God knows he was a man,
And tells him so tonight. Another man
Mixed fear with power and hate and made of it
A poison that was death, and more than death,
And strangled me to make me swallow it—
And here I am. I shall not be here long
To trouble you; and I shall not forget
Your seeing in me a remnant of mankind,
And not a piece of God's peculiar clay
Shaped as a reptile, or as a black snake.
A black man, to be sure; and that's important.

I cannot tell you about God, my friend,
But in my life I have learned more of men
Than would be useful now, or necessary,
If a man's life were only a man's life.
Sometimes it is, or looks to be, no better
Than a weed growing to be crushed or cut,
Or at the most and best, or worst, to live
And shrivel and slowly die and be forgotten.
Others are not like that; and it appears
That mine was not. Mine was a million lives,
And millions after them. Why am I here!
What have I done to die in a cold hole
In a cold land that has no need of me?
Men have been mightier than in doing this thing
To me, I think. Yet who am I to say it?
An exile, buried alive in a cold grave
For serving man, as men may still remember.
There are diseased and senseless ways of hate
That puzzle me—partly because I'm black,
Perhaps, though more because of things that are,
And shall be, and for God may say how long.

Hear me, and I will tell you a strange thing—
Which may be new and of an interest
To many who may not know so much of me
As even my name until my name shall have

A meaning in this world's unhappy story.
Napoleon cannot starve my name to death,
Or blot it out with his. There is an island
Where men remember me; and from an island
Surprising freight of dreams and deeds may come,
To make men think. Is it not strange, my friend—
If you are there—that one dishonored slave,
One animal owned and valued at a price,
One black commodity, should have seen so early
All that I saw? When I filled sight with action,
I could see tyranny's blood-spattered eyes
That saw no farther, laughing at God and fate,
Than a day's end, or possibly one day more,—
Until I made them see. Was it not strange?
Drivers and governors of multitudes
Must be more than themselves, and have more eyes
Than one man's eyes, or scorn will bury them,
Or leave them worse uncovered; and time will pass them
Only to kick their bones. I could see that;
And my prophetic eyes, where God had fixed them
In this black face, could see in front of them
A flaming shambles of men's ignorance
Of all that men should know. I could see farther;
And in a world far larger than my island
Could see the foul indifferent poison wreaking
Sorrow and death and useless indignation
On millions who are waiting to be born;
And this because the few that have the word
Are mostly the wrong few in the wrong places.
On thrones or chairs of state too high for them,
Where they sit swollen or scared, or both, as may be,
They watch, unseen, a diligent see-saw
Played by their privileged and especial slaves
On slippery planks that shake and smell of blood
That flows from crushed and quivering backs and arms
Of slaves that hold them up. There are more slaves
Than have yet felt or are to feel, and know it,
An iron or a lash. This will go on

Until more slaves like me, and more, and more,
Throw off their shackles and make swords of them
For those to feel who have not felt before,
And will not see. It will go on as long
As men capitulate who feel and see,
And men who know say nothing. If this means
It must go on for always—well I have done
All that one man—one black man, I should say—
Could do against a madness and a system
And a malicious policy, all rotten
With craft and hate. It will be so again:
Humanity will hear the lash of scorn
And ignorance again falling on hope,
And hearing it will feel it. Ignorance,
Always a devil, is a father of devils
When it has power and fire and hate to play with,
And goes down with the noise of its own house
Falling, always too late to save itself,
Because it has no eyes. That's power, my friend.
If you are sorry to be born without it,
Be sorry for something else, and answer me:
Is power a breaking down of flesh and spirit?
Is foresight a word lost with a lost language?
Is honor incomprehensible? Is it strange,
That I should sit here and say this to you—
Here in the dark? . . . Nothing to eat or drink,
Nothing to do but die? This is not right. . . .
Hear me, and I will tell you what I saw.

Last night I saw Napoleon in hell.
He was not dead, but I knew where he was,
For there was fire and death surrounding him
Like red coals ringed around a scorpion
To make him sting himself rather than burn.
Napoleon burned. I saw his two hands flaming;
And while I saw him I could see that hate
For me was still alive in his blind eyes.
I was no happier for the sight of him,

For that would not help me; and I had seen
Too much already of crime and fire at work
Before I made an end of it—for him
To make of peace a useless waste and fury.
I have not yet gone mad, for I have known
That I was right. It seems a miracle,
Yet I am not so sure it is a mercy
That I have still my wits and memories
For company in this place. I saw him there,
And his hands that were flaming with a fire
They caught from the same fire that they had lighted.
So fire will act, sometimes, apparently.
Well, there he was, and if I'm not in error,
He will be there again before he dies;
And that will not be medicine here for this.
There is no cure for this, except to die,
And there is nothing left that is worth hating—
Not even the hate of him that kills with hate.
Is it that I am weak—or am I wise?
Can a black man be wise? He would say not.
Having his wisdom, he would have to say it
To keep his hate alive; and without that
He would soon hate the sound of his own name.
Prisons have tongues, and this will all be told;
And it will not sound well when men remember.

Where are you now? Is this another night?
Another day—and now another night?
I do not hear you any more, my friend.
Where are you? Were you ever here at all?
I have been here alone now for too long.
They will not let you come to see me again
Until you come to carry a dead man—
I see it now—out of this cold and darkness
To a place where black and white are dark together.
Nothing to eat or drink—nothing to do
But wait, and die. No, it will not sound well.
Where are you now, my friend? I cannot hear you;

I cannot feel you. Are you dead, perhaps?
I said to you it would be perilous
Not to remember that I'm not a man,
But an imprudent piece of merchandise
To buy and sell—or this time rather to steal;
To catch and steal, and carry from my island
To France, and to this place. And in this place,
Is it not strange, my friend, for me to see
So clearly, and in the dark, more than he sees
Who put me here—as I saw long ago
More than a man could do, till it was done?
Yes, it is done, and cannot be undone.
I know, because I know; and only those
Whose creed and caution has been never to know
Will see in that no reason . . . Yes, I know,
My friend, but I do not know where you are.
If you are here, help me to rise and stand
Once more. I cannot sleep. I cannot see.
Nothing to eat or drink—nothing to see
But night. Good night, my friend—if you are here.

Nothing to see but night—and a long night,
My friend. I hear you now. I hear you moving,
And breathing. I can feel you in the dark,
Although I cannot see you. . . . Is this night?
Or is it morning! No, it is not night—
For now I see. You were a dream, my friend!
Glory to God, who made a dream of you,
And of a place that I believed a prison.
There were no prisons—no Napoleons.
I must have been asleep for a long time.
Now I remember. I was on a ship—
A ship they said was carrying me to France.
Why should I go to France? I must have slept,
And sailed away asleep, and sailed on sleeping.
I am not quite awake; yet I can see
White waves, and I can feel a warm wind coming—
And I can see the sun! . . . This is not France—

This is a ship; and France was never a ship.
France was a place where they were starving me
To death, because a black man had a brain.
I feel the sun! Now we are going faster—
Now I see land—I see land and a mountain!
I see white foam along a sunny shore—
And there's a town. Now there are people in it,
Shouting and singing, waving wild arms at me,
And crowding down together to the water!
You know me—and you knew that I was coming!
O you lost faces! My lost friends! My island!
You knew that I was coming. . . .

                                        You are gone.
Where are you gone? Is this the night again?
I cannot see you now. But you are there—
You are still there. And I know who is here.

ANNANDALE AGAIN

ALMOST as if my thought of him
Had called him from he said not where,
He knocked. I knew him through the door,
And Annandale was waiting there.

Nothing of years or distances,
Or deserts that he may have ranged,
Betrayed him. He was Annandale,
The only man who never changed.

"Do as you must," he said, "and God
Will say that you have done no wrong.
Begin by disappointing me,
And ask where I have been so long.

"What matter's it where I have been,
Or on what mountain or what star?
All places are as much alike
As all men and all women are—

"Which is not much. The best of us
Are curiously unlike the worst;
And for some time, at any rate,
The last shall never be the first.

"Wherefore I leave them, having done
No harm to them, or none to show."—
There was no liking such a man;
You loved him, or you let him go.

"Dreamers who crave a common yoke
For bulls and ewes and elephants
May have it; and my having mine
May be a soothing circumstance

"For you and me, and for my wife;
I mean my new wife Damaris.
I'll tell you, if you must be told,
The sort of woman that she is.

"When Miriam died, my former wife,
I wept and said that all was done;
Yet even as long ago as then
My darkness had a smothered sun

"Behind it, trying to shine through.
More like a living voice of light
It was, than like the sun itself,
And my night was not wholly night.

"And my world was not wholly gone,
As I had feared. Well, hardly so.

I wonder we should learn to live,
Where there's so much for us to know.

"For that, we don't. We live meanwhile;
And then, with nothing learned, we die.
God has been very good to him
Whose end is not an asking why.

"But I'm astray, beginning ill
To lose myself in setting out;
It was my new wife Damaris
That you were asking me about.

"Your interest was an innocence,
And your concern was no surprise.
Well, I have brought her home with me,
And you may find her in my eyes.

"In general, there's no more to tell;
Yet there's this in particular:
She knows the way the good God made
My fur to lie; and there you are.

"And that's enough; you know the rest.
You know as much as I may learn,
Should we go to the end of time
Together, and through time return

"To now again. I should like that,
Ad infinitum. So you see
How graciously has fate prepared
A most agreeable trap for me.

"For where we stay because we must,
Prison or cage or sacrament,
We're in a trap. This world is one,
Obscurely sprung for our ascent,

"Maybe, till we are out of it,
And in another. Once I thought
My cage was dark; but there was light
To let me see that I was caught

"For always there, with Damaris
In the same cage. It's large enough
To hold as many as two of us,
With no constraint worth speaking of.

"The Keeper, who's invisible,
Reveals himself in many a sign,
To caution me that I shall read
And heed the benefits that are mine—

"I don't say hers. Still, if she likes
Her cage with me, and says it's home,
And sings in it, what shall I say
That you may not find wearisome?

"You doctors, who have found so much
In matter that it's hardly there,
May all, in your discomfiture,
Anon be on your knees in prayer

"For larger presence of what is
In what is not. Then you will see
Why Damaris, who knows everything,
Knows how to find so much in me.

"She finds what I have never found
Before; and there's a fearsome doubt,
Sometimes, that slumbers and awaits
A day when Damaris finds out

"How much of undistinguished man
There is in her new destiny.

When she divines it, I shall not
Be told, or not immediately—

"Nor ever, if I'm as amiable
As her attention apprehends.
I'm watching her, and hiding tight
Within me several odds and ends

"Of insights and forbearances
And cautious ways of being kind,
That she has dropped like handkerchiefs,
Conceivably for me to find.

"But one shall not acquire all this
At once, or so it would appear.
I've lain awake establishing
Her permutations in a year—

"Not always indispensable,
You say; and yet, for recompense,
Revealing, when it looks like rain,
A refuge of intelligence;

"Which, with all honor to the rest
That makes a cage enjoyable,
Is not the least of ornaments
That every woman may as well

"Inherit as an amulet
For disillusions unforeseen—
Assuming always that for her
May still be some that have not been.

"Meanwhile, perfection has a price
That humor always has to pay
With patience, as a man may learn
Of woman when she has her way.

"While Miriam lived, I made a book
To make another woman wise.
Blessed are they who are not born
Above instruction by surprise.

"But there was wisdom in it too;
And there are times her eyes are wet
With wonder that I should foresee
So much of her before we met.

"Again, when her complexities
Are restive, or she may have bruised
An elbow on the bars of home,
I may be for a time confused;

"But not for long. She gratifies
A casual need of giving pain;
And having drawn a little blood,
She folds her paws and purrs again.

"So all goes well; and with our wits
Awake, should go indefinitely—
Sufficient without subterfuge,
Harmonious without history.

"You'll find us cheerful prisoners
Enough, with nothing to bewail.
I've told you about Damaris;
And I'll go home."—Poor Annandale!

Poor Damaris! He did not go
So far as home that afternoon.
It may be they offended fate
With harmonies too much in tune

For a discordant earth to share
Unslain, or it may just have been,

Like stars and leaves and marmosets,
Fruition of a force unseen.

There was a sick crash in the street,
And after that there was no doubt
Of what there was; and I was there
To watch while Annandale went out.

No pleasure was awaiting me,
And there would have been none for you;
And mine was the one light I had
To show me the one thing to do.

Sometimes I'll ask myself, alone,
The measure of her debt to me
If some of him were still alive,
And motionless, for her to see;

Sometimes I'll ask if Annandale,
Could he have seen so far ahead,
Had been so sure as I am now
Of more than all he might have said.

I'll ask, and ask, and always ask,
And have no answer; or none yet.
The gain that lives in woman's loss
Is one that woman may forget

For a long time. A doctor knows
The nature of an accident;
And Damaris, who knows everything,
May still be asking what it meant.

THE SPIRIT SPEAKING

(CHRISTMAS, 1929)

As you are still pursuing it
  As blindly as you can,
You have deformed and tortured it
  Since ignorance began;
And even as you have mangled it,
  The Letter has killed man.

Because a camel cannot well
  Go through a needle's eye,
No jealous God has ever said
  The son of man must die;
Only the God that you have made
  Has mocked you from the sky.

No God has in his mightiness
  Told you that love is fear;
And some of you, who are almost
  Too mighty to be here,
May fancy that you are not so—
  If only once a year.

As long as you contend with it
  For longer fear and pain,
As always you have injured it
  And angered it again,
A grief and a malevolence
  The Letter will remain.

THE PRODIGAL SON

You are not merry, brother. Why not laugh,
As I do, and acclaim the fatted calf?
For, unless ways are changing here at home,

You might not have it if I had not come.
And were I not a thing for you and me
To execrate in anguish, you would be
As indigent a stranger to surprise,
I fear, as I was once, and as unwise.
Brother, believe, as I do, it is best
For you that I'm again in the old nest—
Draggled, I grant you, but your brother still,
Full of good wine, good viands, and good will.
You will thank God, some day, that I returned,
And may be singing for what you have learned,
Some other day; and one day you may find
Yourself a little nearer to mankind.
And having hated me till you are tired
You will begin to see, as if inspired,
It was fate's way of educating us.
Remembering then when you were venomous,
You will be glad enough that I am gone,
But you will know more of what's going on;
For you will see more of what makes it go,
And in more ways than are for you to know.
We are so different when we are dead,
That you, alive, may weep for what you said;
And I, the ghost of one you could not save,
May find you planting lentils on my grave.

HECTOR KANE

If Hector Kane at eighty-five
Was not the youngest man alive,
Appearance had anointed him
   With undiminished youth.
To look at him was to believe
That as we ask we may receive,
Annoyed by no such evil whim
   As death, or time, or truth.

Which is to doubt, if any of you,
Seeing him, had believed him true.
He was too young to be so old,
   Too old to be so fair.
Beneath a snowy crown of curls,
His cheeks that might have been a girl's
Were certainly, if truth were told,
   Too rose-like to be there.

But Hector was a child of earth,
And would have held of little worth
Reflection or misgiving cast
   On his reality.
It was a melancholy crime,
No less, to torture life with time;
And whoso did was first and last
   Creation's enemy.

He told us, one convivial night,
When younger men were not so bright
Or brisk as he, how he had spared
   His heart a world of pain,
Merely by seeing always clear
What most it was he wanted here,
And having it when most he cared,
   And having it again.

"You children of threescore or so,"
He said, "had best begin to know
If your infirmities that ache,
   Your lethargies and fears,
And doubts, are mostly more or less
Like things a drunkard in distress
May count with horror, while you shake
   For counting days and years.

"Nothing was ever true for me
Until I found it so," said he;

"So time for me has always been
    Four letters of a word.
Time? Is it anything to eat?
Or maybe it has legs and feet,
To go so as to be unseen;
    Or maybe it's a bird.

"Years? I have never seen such things.
Why let your fancy give them wings
To lift you from experience
    And carry you astray?
If only you will not be old,
Your mines will give you more than gold,
And for a cheerful diligence
    Will keep the worm away.

"We die of what we eat and drink,
But more we die of what we think;
For which you see me still as young
    At heart as heretofore.
So here's to what's awaiting us—
Cras ingens iterabimus—"
A clutch of wonder gripped his tongue,
    And Hector said no more.

Serene and inarticulate
He lay, for us to contemplate.
The mortal trick, we all agreed,
    Was never better turned:
Bequeathing us to time and care,
He told us yet that we were there
To make as much as we could read
    Of all that he had learned.

EDITOR'S NOTE

BIBLIOGRAPHY

INDEX

Editor's Note and Bibliography

The poems in this volume have all been taken from the *Collected Poems* of Edwin Arlington Robinson as published by The Macmillan Company, New York, first in 1921, again in amplified editions in 1927 and 1929, and in a "complete edition with additional poems" in 1937. The present texts follow the complete edition of 1937 in its twelfth printing of 1959.

The poems here selected (with the exception of three poems at the end of the first part of this book, which have been regrouped) follow the sequence of the groups in which Robinson arranged them for the *Collected Poems* of 1929 under the subtitles he carried over into that volume from his individual books of verse. He did not, however, arrange these groups in a chronological order in the *Collected Poems*. He opened the book with *The Man Against the Sky* (1916); followed it with *The Children of the Night* (which he dated 1890–1897), including under this subtitle poems from his first book, *The Torrent and the Night Before* (1896), and from his second, *The Children of the Night* (1897), and its revised edition (1905); then with *Captain Craig, Etc.* (1902), *Merlin* (1917), *The Town Down the River* (1910), *Lancelot* (1920), *The Three Taverns* (1920), *Avon's Harvest, Etc.* (1921), *Tristram* (1927), *Roman Bartholow* (1923), *Dionysus in Doubt* (1925), *The Man Who Died Twice* (1924), and *Cavender's House* (1929), thus bringing the *Collected Poems* down to their 1929 edition. In the edition of *Collected Poems* of 1937, published two years after Robinson's death, his remaining volumes were added in chronological order: *The Glory of the Nightingales* (1930), *Matthias at the Door* (1931), *Nicodemus* (1932), *Talifer* (1933), *Amaranth* (1934), and *King Jasper* (1935). In the present volume, these sections of the *Collected Poems* of 1937 have been arranged in chronological order so far as poems from them have been selected for inclusion. The book-length poems—*Merlin*, *Lancelot*, *Roman Bartholow*, *The Man Who Died Twice*, *Tristram*, *Cavender's House*, *The Glory of the Nightingales*, *Matthias at the Door*, *Talifer*, *Amaranth*, and *King Jasper*—and several long poems virtually of book length, such as "Captain Craig," have had to be omitted because of space limitations.

The texts of the poems follow Robinson's final and authorized texts of the *Collected Poems*. In his earlier years, he sometimes subjected his work to considerable revision when carrying poems over from maga-

247

zine printings to his collective volumes and from one edition to another of these. To cite one familiar example: when the poem "Boston" was first printed in the *Boston Evening Transcript* of October 8, 1896, and then in *The Torrent and the Night Before* in 1896 and again in *The Children of the Night* in 1897, it appeared as a sonnet of fourteen lines; in the 1905 edition of *The Children of the Night,* it was reduced to the eight lines of its octave and was so continued in the *Collected Poems* of 1921 and later editions. Two poems of *The Torrent and the Night Before* ("For Calderon" and "A Poem for Max Nordau") were omitted from *The Children of the Night,* and sixteen new poems were added; of the poems in the latter volume, twelve were omitted from the *Collected Poems* of 1921 ("The Children of the Night," "The Night Before," "The Ballade of Dead Friends," "Ballade of the White Ship," "For a Book by Thomas Hardy," "For Some Poems by Matthew Arnold," "Walt Whitman," "Kosmos," "The Miracle," "The World," "Romance," and "Two Octaves"). Certain other poems, among them "Captain Craig," "Octaves," and "The House on the Hill," were considerably revised, shortened, or lengthened. A good many incidental revisions were made in the first *Collected Poems* of 1921, and some appeared between magazine and book publication as late as the 1920's. A study of these revisions requires the consultation of Robinson's serial printings, his first and subsequent editions of individual volumes, and the later collected editions. The bibliographies by Hogan and Lippincott, cited below, are indispensable in this matter. From the time of the first *Collected Poems* in 1921, and particularly after its amplified edition of 1927, Robinson generally allowed his poems to stand in the versions there established.

INDIVIDUAL VOLUMES AND COLLECTIONS

The Torrent and the Night Before (Cambridge, Mass.: Riverside Press, 1896). Privately printed for the author.

The Children of the Night (Boston: Richard G. Badger, 1897). This carries over most of the poems, sometimes revised of *The Torrent and the Night Before,* with additions.

Captain Craig: A Book of Poems (Boston and New York: Houghton Mifflin, 1902).

The Town Down the River: A Book of Poems (New York: Scribner, 1910).

Van Zorn: A Comedy in Three Acts (New York: Macmillan, 1914).

Captain Craig: A Book of Poems (New York: Macmillan, 1915). Revised edition with additional poems.

The Porcupine: A Drama in Three Acts (New York: Macmillan, 1915).

The Man Against the Sky: A Book of Poems (New York: Macmillan, 1916).

Merlin: A Poem (New York: Macmillan, 1917).

Lancelot: A Poem (New York: Thomas Seltzer, 1920).

The Three Taverns: A Book of Poems (New York: Macmillan, 1920).

Avon's Harvest (New York: Macmillan, 1921).

Collected Poems (New York: Macmillan, 1921). This collected edition was also issued in a limited signed paper edition in two volumes by the Brick Row Bookshop, New York, New Haven, and Princeton, in 1921.

Roman Bartholow (New York: Macmillan, 1923).

The Man Who Died Twice (New York: Macmillan, 1924).

Dionysus in Doubt: A Book of Poems (New York: Macmillan, 1925).

Tristram (New York: Macmillan, 1927). Also issued in a subscriber's edition by the Literary Guild, New York, 1927.

Collected Poems (New York: Macmillan, 1927). This five-volume edition of the *Collected Poems*, through *Tristram* of 1927, was also issued in a signed paper edition of 300 sets by Dunster House, Cambridge, Mass., in 1927. The sequence of Robinson's individual books of poems differs in this edition from that of the collected editions of 1929 and 1937.

The Torrent and the Night Before (New York, New Haven, Princeton: Brick Row Bookshop, 1928). A limited signed edition of 110 copies of Robinson's first book.

Three Poems Two short poems originally printed in *The Harvard Advocate* of October 16 and December 11, 1891, and a theretofore unpublished fragment of "Lancelot," later used by Robinson in *Modred*, 1929. A pirated edition, "printed without the author's permission or knowledge," 15 copies, no publisher named, was issued in Cambridge, Mass., in May, 1928.

Sonnets: 1889–1927 (New York: Macmillan, 1928).

Fortunatus (Reno, Nev.: Slide Mountain Press, 1928). Printed by the Grabhorn Press, San Francisco, 171 copies.

Modred: A Fragment (New York, New Haven, and Princeton: Brick Row Bookshop, 1929).

Cavender's House (New York: Macmillan, 1929).

Collected Poems (New York: Macmillan, 1929). The contents of the 1927 *Collected Poems*, with the addition of *Cavender's House*.

The Prodigal Son (New York: Random House, 1929). The single poem was issued as one of the Poetry Quartos, 475 copies.

The Valley of the Shadow (San Francisco: Yerba Buena Press, 1930).

The Glory of the Nightingales (New York: Macmillan, 1930).

Poems (New York: Macmillan, 1931). Selected and with a preface by Bliss Perry.

Matthias at the Door (New York: Macmillan, 1931).

Nicodemus: A Book of Poems (New York: Macmillan, 1932).

Talifer (New York: Macmillan, 1933).

Amaranth (New York: Macmillan, 1934).

King Jasper (New York: Macmillan, 1935). Introduction by Robert Frost.

Hannibal Brown (Buffalo, New York: M. Klinke, 1936). Published posthumously.

Collected Poems (New York: Macmillan, 1937). Complete edition, including all of the previous *Collected Poems*, with the addition of the later poems through and including *King Jasper*. Twelfth printing, 1959.

Tilbury Town: Selected Poems of Edwin Arlington Robinson (New York: Macmillan, 1953). Introduction and notes by Lawrance Thompson.

Selected Early Poems and Letters (New York: Holt, 1960). Edited and with an Introduction by Charles T. Davis.

BIBLIOGRAPHIES

Beebe, Lucius, and Robert J. Bulkley, Jr., *A Bibliography of the Writings of Edwin Arlington Robinson* (Cambridge, Mass.: Dunster House Bookshop, 1931).

Hogan, Charles Beecher, *A Bibliography of the Writings of Edwin Arlington Robinson* (New Haven, Conn.: Yale University Press, 1936). Later supplements have been issued.

Lippincott, Lillian, *A Bibliography of the Writings and Criticisms of Edwin Arlington Robinson* (Boston: F. W. Faxon, 1937).

A Literary History of the United States, edited by Robert E. Spiller, Willard Thorp, Thomas H. Johnson, and Henry Seidel Canby, Volume III: *Bibliography* (New York: Macmillan, 1948), pp. 705–708. This bibliography is continued through 1957 in a *Bibliography Supplement*, edited by Richard M. Ludwig (New York: Macmillan, 1959), pp. 184–185.

BIOGRAPHIES AND MEMOIRS

Bates, Esther Willard, *Edwin Arlington Robinson and His Manuscripts* (Waterville, Me.: Colby College Library, 1944).

Brown, Rollo Walter, *Next Door to a Poet* (New York: Appleton-Century, 1937).

Hagedorn, Hermann, *Edwin Arlington Robinson* (New York: Macmillan, 1939). A major, full-length biography of Robinson.

Neff, Emery, *Edward Arlington Robinson* (New York: Sloane, 1948). Includes extensive interpretation of the poetry also.

Richards, Laura E., *E. A. R.* (Cambridge, Mass.: Harvard University Press, 1936). Includes reminiscences of Robinson by friends of his youth and later life.

Robinson, Edwin Arlington, "The First Seven Years," in *The Colophon*, December, 1930; included in *Breaking Into Print* (New York: Simon and Schuster, 1937).

—— *Selected Letters* (New York: Macmillan, 1940). Introduction by Ridgely Torrence.

—— *Untriangulated Stars: Letters of Edwin Arlington Robinson to Harry de Forest Smith: 1890–1905* (Cambridge, Mass.: Harvard University Press, 1947). Edited by Denham Sutcliffe.

Smith, Chard Powers, *Where the Light Falls,* (New York: Macmillan, 1965).

Shorter accounts of Robinson's life are included in some of the books listed below—those by Lloyd R. Morris (1923), Ben Ray Redman (1926), Mark Van Doren (1927), Yvor Winters (1946), Edwin Sill Fussell (1954)—and there are various short memoirs by various friends of Robinson in magazines. Other letters have been published, *e.g.*, Daniel Gregory Mason, "Early Letters of Edwin Arlington Robinson," *Virginia Quarterly Review*, Spring, 1937; *Letters of E. A. Robinson to Howard G. Schmitt*, edited by Carl J. Weber (Waterville, Me.: Colby College Library, 1943). Further bibliographical aid is provided by Edith J. R. Isaacs and Léonie Adams in "The Ledoux Collection of Edwin Arlington Robinson," *Library of Congress Quarterly Journal*, November, 1949, and by other investigators. Collections of Robinson papers, manuscripts, and letters are in the Harvard College Library, the Library of Congress, the Princeton University Library, the Williams College Library, the Alderman Library of the University of Virginia, the Colby College Library, the University of Maine Library, and others.

CRITICISM AND INTERPRETATION

Books on Robinson:

*Barnard, Ellsworth, *Edwin Arlington Robinson: A Critical Study* (New York: Macmillan, 1952).

251

*Betsky, Seymour, *Some Aspects of the Philosophy of Edwin Arlington Robinson: Self-Knowledge, Self-Acceptance, and Conscience.* Harvard University dissertation, 1942, unpublished.

Cestre, Charles, *An Introduction to Edwin Arlington Robinson* (New York: Macmillan, 1930).

*Dauner, Louise, *Studies in Edwin Arlington Robinson.* State University of Iowa dissertation, 1944, unpublished.

*Fussell, Edwin Sill, *Edwin Arlington Robinson: The Literary Background of a Traditional Poet* (Berkeley, Calif.: University of California Press, 1954).

*Kaplan, Estelle, *Philosophy in the Poetry of Edwin Arlington Robinson* (New York: Columbia University Press, 1940).

Morris, Lloyd R., *The Poetry of Edwin Arlington Robinson* (New York: Doran, 1923).

*Neff, Emery, *Edwin Arlington Robinson* (New York: Sloane, 1948).

Redman, Ben Ray, *Edwin Arlington Robinson* (New York: McBride, 1926).

*Smith, Chard Powers, *Where the Light Falls: A Portrait of Edwin Arlington Robinson* (New York: Macmillan, 1965).

Van Doren, Mark, *Edwin Arlington Robinson* (New York: Literary Guild of America, 1927).

*Winters, Yvor, *Edwin Arlington Robinson* (Norfolk, Conn., and New York: New Directions Books, 1946).

Asterisks indicate books of special value.

Selected Essays and Articles

Aiken, Conrad, *A Reviewer's ABC: Collected Criticism of Conrad Aiken from 1916 to the Present* (New York: Meridian Books, 1958).

Blackmur, R. P., "Verse That Is Too Easie," *Poetry*, January, 1934.

Bogan, Louise, "Tilbury Town and Beyond," *Poetry*, January, 1931.

—— *Selected Criticism* (New York: Noonday Press, 1955).

Brooks, Van Wyck, *New England: Indian Summer* (New York: Dutton, 1940).

Brown, David, "E. A. Robinson's Later Poems," *New England Quarterly*, X (1937), pp. 487–502.

Carpenter, Frederick I., "Tristram the Transcendent," *New England Quarterly*, September, 1938.

Colum, Mary M., "Poets and Their Problems," *The Forum*, June, 1935.

Cowley, Malcolm, "Edwin Arlington Robinson: Defeat and Triumph," *The New Republic*, December 6, 1948.

Coxe, Louis O., "E. A. Robinson: The Lost Tradition," *Sewanee Review,* LXII (1954), pp. 247–266.

Crowder, Richard, "E. A. Robinson's Symphony: 'The Man Who Died Twice,'" *College English,* XI (1949), pp. 141–144.

—— "'The Man Against the Sky,'" *College English,* XIV (1953), pp. 269–276.

Dauner, Louise, "Avon and Cavender: Two Children of the Night," *American Literature,* March, 1942.

—— "Vox Clamantis: Edwin Arlington Robinson As a Critic of Democracy," *New England Quarterly,* September, 1942.

Evans, Nancy, "Edwin Arlington Robinson," *The Bookman,* November, 1932.

Frost, Robert, Introduction to *King Jasper,* by Edwin Arlington Robinson (New York: Macmillan, 1935).

Gorman, Herbert S., "Edwin Arlington Robinson," *The New Republic,* February 19, 1922.

Gregory, Horace, and Marya Zaturenska, *A History of American Poetry: 1900–1940* (New York: Harcourt, Brace, 1946).

Hudson, Hoyt H., "Robinson and Praed," *Poetry,* February, 1943.

Lowell, Amy, *Tendencies in Modern American Poetry* (New York: Macmillan, 1917).

Monroe, Harriet, *Poets and Their Art* (New York: Macmillan, 1926).

—— "Robinson As Man and Poet," *Poetry,* June, 1935.

Munson, Gorham B., *Destinations* (New York: J. H. Sears, 1928).

Ransom, John Crowe, "Autumn of Poetry," *The Southern Review,* Winter, 1936.

Roosevelt, Theodore, "The Children of the Night," *The Outlook,* August, 1905.

Scott, Winfield Townley, "The Unaccredited Profession," *Poetry,* June, 1937.

—— "Robinson to Robinson," *Poetry,* May, 1939.

—— "To See Robinson," *The New Mexico Quarterly,* XXVI (1956), pp. 161–178.

Stovall, Floyd, "The Optimism Behind Robinson's Tragedies," *American Literature,* March, 1938.

Sutcliffe, Denham, "The Original of Robinson's Captain Craig," *New England Quarterly,* September, 1943.

Tate, Allen, "Again, O Ye Laurels," *The New Republic,* October, 1933.

—— *Reactionary Essays on Poetry and Ideas* (New York: Putnam, 1936).

Waggoner, Hyatt Howe, "E. A. Robinson and the Cosmic Chill," *New England Quarterly,* XIII (1940), pp. 65–84.

Wells, Henry W., *New Poets from Old* (New York: Columbia University Press, 1940).

Whipple, T. K., *Spokesmen* (New York: Appleton, 1928).

Winters, Yvor, "Religious and Social Ideas in the Didactic Work of E. A. Robinson," *Arizona Quarterly*, I (1945), pp. 70–85.

Zabel, Morton Dauwen, "Robinson in America," *Poetry*, June, 1935.

—— "Robinson," under "Four Poets in America," *Literary Opinion in America* (New York: Harper, 1937).

—— "Robinson: The Ironic Discipline," *The Nation*, August 28, 1937.

Some of the material in the last three essays listed above has been adapted for the Introduction to the present volume by the editor.

Index of Titles

255